CAPTURE THE MINDSHARE AND THE MARKET SHARE WILL FOLLOW

THE ART AND SCIENCE OF BUILDING BRANDS

LIBBY GILL

palgrave
macmillan

First published in 2013 by PALGRAVE MACMILLAN® in the
United States—a division of St. Martin's Press LLC, 175 Fifth Avenue,
New York, NY 10010.

Where this book is distributed in the UK, Europe and the rest of the world,
this is by Palgrave Macmillan, a division of Macmillan Publishers Limited,
registered in England, company number 785998, of Houndmills,
Basingstoke, Hampshire RG21 6XS.

Palgrave Macmillan is the global academic imprint of the above companies
and has companies and representatives throughout the world.

Palgrave® and Macmillan® are registered trademarks in the United States,
the United Kingdom, Europe and other countries.

ISBN 978–1–137–27851–7

Library of Congress Cataloging-in-Publication Data

Gill, Libby.
    Capture the mindshare and the market share will follow : the art and
science of building brands / Libby Gill.
      pages cm
    ISBN 978–1–137–27851–7 (alk. paper)
    1. Branding (Marketing) 2. Business communication—Psychological
aspects. I. Title.

HF5415.1255.G55 2013
658.8′27—dc23   2013003483

A catalogue record of the book is available from the British Library.

Design by Newgen KnowledgeWorks

First edition: August 2013

10 9 8 7 6 5 4 3 2 1

Printed in the United States of America.

CONTENTS

To the beloved men in my life—Harrison, Zack, and now David. You have captured my heart.

ACKNOWLEDGMENTS

WHEN IT COMES TO BRANDING, I ALWAYS THINK IT'S MORE important to be clear than clever. So I'll forgo cleverness here and instead offer my utmost gratitude to the people who add so much to my work and life.

I am beyond fortunate to collaborate with the literary trifecta of James Levine, Kerry Sparks, and Laurie Harting, as well as all the good folks at Palgrave. Many thanks for your hard work, talent, and dedication.

Big hugs and heartfelt thanks to Martha Finney, my literary comrade and advisor. You have enriched my life more than you know. Thanks to Carolyn Akel, a great friend and business partner, who makes work more fun than I ever thought possible. And to my cheerleaders and readers: Wendy Winks, Shela Dean, Belinda Phillips, and Sharon Williams—what would I do without you? And a super-special thank you to Rachel Kane, who has been an enormous support throughout this process.

To my mom, Barbara Burgess, who had to put up with me— which wasn't always easy—and my brother Cameron Chambers, an incredibly talented author and teacher. I love you both.

Finally, to all my clients and colleagues who so graciously shared your stories of challenge, change, and hope. I am in your debt.

INTRODUCTION

BUSINESS IS BUILT ON CAPTURING THE MARKET SHARE. BUT THE most successful individuals and organizations know that before they win the market share, they must *capture the mindshare*—that is, the heads, hearts, trust, and loyalty—of their customers. *Capture the Mindshare* looks past the profit and loss reports to reveal how great companies succeed by creating authentic connections with their customers, clients, and colleagues, as well as with their own workforce.

This book will provide a blueprint for building deep and lasting connections for anyone who needs to influence, attract, persuade, or sell. *Capture the Mindshare* is for executives and entrepreneurs, emerging leaders, and established stars—basically anyone who strives to build a cutting-edge brand in a cluttered landscape, create inspired connections with customers, or propel employees to higher levels of achievement.

Capture the Mindshare is about the art and science of building brands, whether you're running a small business, heading a Fortune 500 company, or located somewhere in between. This book is designed to elevate the conversation about branding—which is, after all, simply the art of maintaining an ongoing connection—by addressing what I believe should be the focus of any enterprise: to create awareness; provide authentic value; motivate others to act; and build long-term loyalty based on hope, trust, and respect.

Sound like a big challenge? Well, yes...and no. Chances are you're ticking a lot of those boxes already. You wouldn't be reading this book if defining your brand promise and delivering on it weren't of paramount importance to you. But my guess is that you want to do an even better job than you're already doing. And that's where I can help. As a business coach and brand strategist, I've worked with clients as far ranging as the French government, where I help entrepreneurs refine their brands for the North American marketplace, and leaders at companies such as Disney, Nike, and PayPal, where I've guided people to enhance their executive brands. My goal is to help you define your unique value and articulate your *mindshare brand* by providing you with a replicable, step-by-step process for inspiring loyalty based on business *and* emotion.

Capture the Mindshare will explore why we connect, with whom we connect, where we connect, and, most of all, *how* we connect. Sometimes this connection is made with words in person or online. Sometimes it's made with physical behavior, appearance, or visual images. And sometimes it's a more elusive emotional connection that drives the relationship. *Capture the Mindshare* will explore all of these ways of connecting with others, from the scientific concepts of neuromarketing to the practical tools of communication so you can begin expanding your brand today.

I'll share a multitude of methods by which you can connect, influence, or persuade someone to do something. The *something*—that is, the action you want your end user to take after you make the connection—is entirely up to you. I'll simply help you broaden your options and opportunities for making those meaningful mindshare connections. This book is specifically designed for the influencers—and potential influencers—of the world who want to take their business to a more significant level in terms of reach and value. Perhaps you fit into one of these influencer categories:

- The leader striving to create a culture of engagement and productivity

- The entrepreneur seeking a competitive edge within her industry
- The manager looking to open his business division to new markets
- The consultant eager to establish new relationships
- The marketer searching for fresh perspective and inspiration
- The community activist or non-profit attempting to promote positive change

I first encountered the concepts now collectively referred to as *branding* during my first career as a Hollywood studio executive at Sony Pictures Entertainment, Universal Television, and Turner Broadcasting, where I oversaw media relations, publicity, and promotional campaigns on scores of television series like *Married...with Children*, *Law & Order*, *Xena: Warrior Princess*, *Dr. Phil*, *Who's the Boss?*, *Ricki Lake*, and many more. In my various professional roles helping to shape pop culture and public perception, I became a student of what motivates people to buy, hire, watch, listen, or read. What I saw time and time again was that not only does perception often create reality, but it also generates box office grosses, Nielsen ratings, CD sales, and, occasionally, overnight celebrity. I observed that if you could create enough of an emotional connection in the minds of the audience—building on a well-sculpted image—you could often turn that perceived image into reality. (Could *Xena* ever have found her way into *Time* magazine, the *Wall Street Journal*, and the *Tonight Show* as a female action icon any other way?) And yet perception could occasionally be misleading, like a film that gets great advance "buzz" because of the star or director but is declared dead on arrival by the audience after the first weekend.

It was folly, I learned, to underestimate the audience, and I still firmly believe that, despite an overall dumbing down of America that continues to concern me. Still, for the most part, we know when we're being sold crap, and we also know when we are being treated to genius. And while one can appreciate the goofiness of *Dumb and Dumber* or *Jerry Springer* (a show I worked on during its wacky, chair-throwing heyday), more people are likely to connect with the heart of the *Oprah Winfrey Show* or the passion of *Jerry Maguire*.

It's no different in the business world. When you consistently share authentic value with your colleagues and customers, respect, trust, and loyalty naturally follow. If you're failing to articulate your value in a meaningful and memorable way that separates you from the pack, or if you're not providing consistent value over time, then you've got a big problem on your hands. You better figure out the disconnect—fast—because your competitors already have.

NAVIGATING THE SEVEN CORE MINDSHARE METHODS

Throughout the following seven chapters, using case studies and client success stories as examples, you'll learn how to define and articulate your brand. You'll master my *Seven Core Mindshare Methods* of *Clarify, Commit, Collaborate, Connect, Compete, Communicate,* and *Contribute.* My brand promise to you is that as you layer one concept upon the next, trying bold new actions as you go, you'll be building competence and confidence. And as you begin to differentiate yourself in the competitive landscape by promising and delivering unique value, you will see relationships deepen, opportunities expand, and careers flourish. Read on, drill down, and discover the art and science of capturing the mindshare.

Chapter One

CLARIFY

Discovering Your Emotional Assignment

I want to make a dent in the universe.

—*Steve Jobs*

FOR NEARLY 100 YEARS, ALL SOULS COLLEGE AT OXFORD GAVE applicants what was considered to be one of the most arduous entrance exams in academia: three hours to write an essay based on a single noun. The purpose of the assignment was clear: to showcase one's knowledge and mental agility using a word like *water* or *harmony* as a linguistic springboard. Yet the seemingly simple assignment left plenty to the imagination of the aspirants. It was up to them to creatively connect the dots between the word itself and their value as graduate candidates. More specifically, it was their ability to *capture the mindshare*—that is, the heads and hearts—of the judging panel that would deem them worthy (or not) of admission.

For some, this essay-as-application presented an unbelievably daunting challenge in how to sum up the history and significance of just one word while qualifying them for admission. For others, it provided an opportunity to highlight their strategic thinking and communication skills, delivering a thoughtful brief based on a specific, and often narrow, topic. For all, it demanded crystal clear strategy and language that were compelling enough to smoke the competition.

Your brand deserves no less. In this chapter, we'll explore why *clarity*—of purpose, value, and promise—is the foundation of all great brands, and why the failure to clearly articulate that message, for yourself as well as others, can spell disaster for entrepreneurs and executives, for-profit and non-profit organizations.

DO I REALLY NEED A BRAND?

That's a question that, even in this era of shameless hype, I still get asked on a regular basis. Why, if I consistently offer great value to customers and clients, do I need to think about having a brand, let alone actually taking the time to craft one? Why, indeed.

First, it seems only fair for me to give you my definition of branding, which I don't believe needs to be as overcomplicated or oversimplified as it often is. Jeff Bezos, founder of Amazon.com, reportedly once said, "Your brand is what people say about you when you leave the room." Not a bad definition, actually. Your brand *is* what people say, think, and feel about you and your company. But more than that, your brand is, or should be, a promise of value artfully articulated across multiple platforms. It's obvious, particularly in today's world, where we are bombarded with hundreds, if not thousands, of daily branding messages, that your brand is much more than a logo, name, billboard, marketing campaign, sales sheet, or website. All of those things are, in fact, expressions of your brand and a critical means of connecting and communicating with your customers, but they are only part of the brand story.

Above all, your brand is a promise of value, and the most successful brands—the ones I call *Mindshare brands*—are those that consistently deliver or over-deliver on that value promise over time. Think Coca-Cola. Think Mercedes. Think Apple. Think any brand about which you feel an emotional connection and that you count on to deliver what you want every single time—or pretty darn close to that. Even the big guys slip up occasionally, though well-handled mistakes can actually be terrific branding opportunities.

So why do you have to define your brand? Isn't what you do obvious from the actual doing or delivering of it? Won't your ideal clients and customers find you if you're doing a good job? And doesn't your team inherently understand your internal culture and external brand just by working alongside you? You'd think so, wouldn't you? But we've all known that great neighborhood cafe or web designer or even airline that simply couldn't attract enough, or the right, customers to stay in business without an easily recognizable set of attributes.

If you don't define your brand, the world will simply assign one to you. Even if you are fortunate enough to get "discovered" by your ideal customers, letting them define your brand limits you to their perceptions. And which would you rather have: A brand that is carefully, thoughtfully, strategically crafted and carried out based on your core beliefs and authentic value? Or a brand that the world has deemed is who you are and what you are capable of providing to others? Your brand is your destiny, and if you fail to define, refine, and manage it, you do so at your peril.

PURPOSE, PREMISE, AND PROMISE

It's important first to drill down to the core purpose of your business. Some marketers call this statement of purpose your "value proposition." I prefer to go a little deeper. Ask yourself: Why are you in business in the first place? What is it you actually do? What have you accomplished so far? Even if your business is complex and layered, it still has a core purpose. Amazon.com, so named by Bezos because he wanted a company as vast as the Amazon River, delivers a huge array of items ordered online. The company used to be known for books, especially those that your local bookstore never seemed to have in stock and Amazon always did. Now, its expanded core purpose is to provide the customer with a wide-ranging selection of products, from flat-screen TVs to natural foods to camera equipment, all of which can be researched, ordered, and paid for on their user-friendly website.

The *premise* takes the idea of core purpose a step further. What pain or problem do you solve in the marketplace? In Amazon's case, the company makes one-stop shopping easy, no matter where you live or what stores you have access to. Maybe you save people's lives by inventing drugs that treat hereditary diseases, like pharmaceutical company Regeneron. Or maybe you help busy people get fit and healthy through time-efficient training and nutrition regimens, like my client (and personal trainer) MonicaNelsonFitness.com.

Finally, and this may be the most important factor of all, what is the promise of change that you give your end user? This applies to internal customers, like your staff or management, as well as external consumers. What is the outcome that they can expect from their relationship with you, your services, or your products? What specific results can you promise them because of your expertise and skill? Take Monica Nelson, for example. Her purpose is to help people look and feel healthier. Her premise is that she can provide exercise efficiency and easy nutrition for busy professional people who can't (or won't) spend a lot of time working out or making healthy meals. And her promise—your anticipated outcome—is that you will lose weight, gain muscle mass, look more toned, and feel more energetic.

How you prove that three-pronged hypothesis to your potential customers is a critical part of building your *credibility story*. For now, let's stay focused on your purpose, premise, and promise.

MINDSHARE MINUTE: DEVELOPING YOUR PURPOSE, PREMISE, AND PROMISE

Throughout this book, you'll find downloadable tools to provide strategies to help you capture the mindshare in mere moments. Go online now to www.LibbyGill.com and download the Developing Your Purpose, Premise, & Promise PDF worksheet for more help on your value proposition.

BUILDING BLOCK #1: NAMES THAT SUPPORT YOUR BRAND

Although it's likely that your business or the company you work for already has a name, that doesn't mean that you're through with the naming process. You may be charged with naming a project, team, corporate initiative, blog, campaign, community activity, book, or just about anything else at some point in your career. Names can be critically important and shouldn't be taken for granted. Some names not only tell you who the company is and what they do but also provide an attitude, a tone, or even a specific promise.

Although there are few hard and fast rules for naming—and often you don't know if you've got a great name until it has stood the test of time—you can do some things to increase your odds of landing on a name that supports your brand. Check out these suggestions:

- **Say who you are.** When possible, it's a great idea to encapsulate the value proposition of the enterprise into the name. We immediately get the gist, if not the whole picture, of Whole Foods or Boston Consulting Group. Even company names that play with words, like Zappos (a pun on the Spanish word *zapatos* for shoes) or Italiatour, can say a lot about their business with just their names.
- **Combine clarity and cleverness.** Although I almost always advocate for being clear over being clever, you don't want your name to be dull or boring. Conveying a sense of energy, enthusiasm, and personality can lay the groundwork for telling your clients how to feel about you, like Krispy Kreme or CharityBuzz.

- **Make it sticky.** Think about how memorable your name is. Can people recall it a day or two after you've told them what it is? Can they spell it? Does it make sense both when spoken and when written? How about when you add a dotcom or other web extension after it? Once you've done some brainstorming, think back to your list of proposed names—including the good, the bad, and the ugly—and see how you feel about them. You may be surprised to see what names have stuck with you or sparked additional usable ideas.

- **Short is sweet.** When it comes to naming, size matters and short is better. Short names are generally easier to remember than long ones and often look better on websites and printed materials. Be sure to check BetterWhoIs. com or other domain-buying websites to find out whether the URL of your name is available. I recommend that you buy several variations of it, including misspellings, so that you can redirect users to your site if online searchers get the name wrong.

- **Create a word.** Eventually, you'll be creating a whole brand language, so why not start with your name? The advantage of creating a name from scratch is that it will likely be easier to acquire a URL and trademark (which you'll need to clear with a copyright attorney or through USPTO.gov), since it's unlikely a made-up word will already be in use. The disadvantage is that the name may require some ongoing explanation and awareness building before it sticks, since it may be unfamiliar or obscure to potential users. Some well-known businesses like Google, Verizon, and Skype created unique names by combining words in unusual ways. Google founders Larry Page and Sergey Brin joked that their online search engine could search for a *googol* of information, or the equivalent of the number *one* followed by 100 zeros. Verizon was a combination of the word *veritas*, Latin for truth, and *horizon*. And Skype was originally dubbed Sky-Peer-to-Peer and eventually shortened to the relatively sticky Skype.

As part of my work, I've helped name products, book titles, service packages, and a couple of companies. But I'd never been involved in naming an online dating service until I was asked to join the advisory board of the then-titled start-up TheComplete.me, still in the early throes of the branding process. CEO Brian Bowman, a Match.com pioneer who met his wife through the service and considers Match an integral part of both his personal and professional success, was passionate about bringing an updated model to consumers.[1] A believer in what he calls "radical transparency," Bowman was open about sharing the challenges involved in the branding process, which most start-ups keep to themselves, preferring to have their company names, taglines, and mission statements magically spring from the ether onto their home pages.

Despite their obvious success, Bowman believed that Match.com, like many companies, had fallen victim to an outdated model. Make that *outdated models* plural, since Match.com owns more than two dozen dating sites, and many customers are actually on multiple Match sites without even knowing it. Match.com, as well as most of the dating sites that followed in their online footsteps, was based on a premise of anonymity, not just because people were embarrassed to be discovered dating online, but because their revenue model required that they keep identities secret, since they only received payment when someone was willing to pony up for an online introduction.

Given that dating is a "high-need activity," Bowman says that most people, especially the newly divorced and late bloomers, were willing to pay to play. The problem? Once you met someone, you were through with the service. A successful interaction meant that the company lost the customer and would constantly have to be on the hunt for new prospects and/or wait around until their customers became single again. Undaunted by the challenge and still a fan of the industry, Bowman realized that dating had changed but the industry hadn't kept up—and he set out to solve that problem (remember the idea of market pain?). He created an online service based on "truth and transparency" that extended beyond dating to allow users to set up their single friends and meet new people and business prospects. The *purpose* of the business—to create a better way for people to meet—was backed by a core *premise* of transparency in a heretofore-secretive process. Add to these a distinctive customer *promise*—that meeting people would be fun and easy—and you've got an entirely new take on an existing model. Suggests Bowman, "People shouldn't have to create a dating profile from scratch when who they really are already exists online through their social media." Not only would the new model make it easier for the user to draw from existing sources, it would be inherently more authentic, since there would be no artificial profile constructed merely for the purpose of snagging a date.

Not surprisingly, given his community-building background, Bowman is a big believer in leveraging existing pools of people. With the robustness of Facebook, Twitter, LinkedIn, and other platforms, this new service would promote authenticity (assuming that people are more authentic on social media sites than they are on dating sites) and maximize growth by piggybacking on these mega-communities.

Although Bowman considers clarity of customer value proposition extremely important, he cautions other businesses not to get overly hung up on the name. Sure, it's important, he agrees, but even more important is the user experience. Is it what was promised? Is it satisfying? Does it deliver? Has it been described properly? As he says, the process is iterative and ongoing. Fortunately, great low-cost tools like UserTesting.com (there's a name that says what it is!) will test your website and/or business premise for you. And SurveyMonkey. com not only runs surveys online, as the catchy name suggests, but will also collect basic research data for you.

VICE PRESIDENT OF FIRST IMPRESSIONS

Now that you've nailed down the value proposition (purpose + premise + promise) and possibly even the name of your company, you're half-way home, right? Hardly. Now the real work begins…right at the beginning. Because once you've gotten your customers' attention, that very first interaction you have with them can often be the make-or-break impression that determines whether they want to continue the relationship. One glance at your website, one direct mail marketing piece, or even one phone call creates a lasting impression.

A web designer I know refers to his receptionist as Vice President of First Impressions, since even her mood when she answers the phone can set the tone for how the customer feels about the entire company, justified or not. Successful branders know that it's not only the big-picture vision but also the smallest of details that create the sum total of the customer experience and determine whether you create a fanatic tribe of brand evangelists or a lukewarm pool of prospects that find you, well, forgettable.

I'll give you an example of how one company's thoughtless handling of their brand turned off a potential customer right from the get-go. My colleague Marcy is a devotee of high-end skincare and spa products. When the company from which she regularly buys her fancy skincare items asked whether she would participate in a consumer research study by giving them feedback on a new line of bath soaps, she eagerly jumped at the chance. But when Marcy received their package of soaps, each enclosed in a separate plastic bag with an ID number for a label, she took one look and threw the whole batch under her bathroom sink, never to be retrieved.

Marcy told me this story during a discussion about "repackaging" her own brand as a human resources specialist, drawing a connection between her efforts to remake herself as a professionally relevant consultant and the skincare company's complete neglect of its image. As she said, "The soaps looked so boring in their uninspired little plastic bags, I had no desire to try them. I just thought, if they don't care enough about their product to make them enticing, why should I care?" Good question.

It's no surprise that the cardinal rule of branding—either products or people—is *don't be boring*. But Marcy was already a loyal customer who had a long history with this company. Shouldn't that have been enough to get her to at least sample the products? Obviously not. The total lack of emotional involvement caused her to dump the soaps and could easily cause your customers to dump you. To put it even more bluntly, it's your job to instruct your customers how to feel about you, your products, and your services.

With their casual treatment of their new product—which should have been hailed as their latest and greatest innovation, even if clad in the simplest of packaging—the company told Marcy to treat them offhandedly. They essentially invited her to ignore them. Had the soap folks set up an expectation by telling Marcy that the product would be unmarked, specifically so she wouldn't be influenced; or that because she was a long-time customer, her feedback was more valuable than anyone else's; or even that they had had some trouble developing the products and really needed her help— maybe, just maybe, she would have had a more positive reaction.

But she was less inclined to help this company out, even with the promise of free soap down the line, than you might be if a stranger at the airport asked you to watch his suitcase while he grabbed a Starbucks. Marcy felt no sense of obligation, she experienced no visual hook, and she established no relationship with the soap-filled bags. In short, the soap company failed to create an emotional connection—the kiss of death for brands.

Could the company have bounced back from Marcy's lackluster reaction and limited potential as a customer? Of course, no one interaction is going to break the bank. But multiply that by dozens, thousands, or millions of bad call-center experiences, subpar products, or damaged shipments, and your customers are bound to find an alternative. Because you aren't the only game in town. And if you are, the pressure is on, because it won't be long before others will be right behind you to steal your ideas and capture your customers.

So how do you flip your customer's buy switch from "So what?" to "I've got to have it"? What can you learn from the big guys of branding, like Apple, Walmart, and Coca-Cola, with their gazillion-dollar marketing budgets? And how can you establish the kind of connections that brands like Trader Joe's, Nordstrom, and Gilt Groupe are so good at creating? Our behaviors and buying decisions are based far more on emotion than logic. So it's those all-important moments of emotional connection that really count.

Here are some of the primary reasons people buy:

- **To feel good.** Most human emotions are divided between the desire to increase pleasure and the desire to avoid pain. Brands that make us feel good can actually cause brain chemicals like oxytocin and serotonin to be released into our systems. These brands may evoke a feeling of community (Starbucks), luxury (Rolex), comfort (Keds), or well-being (Whole Foods).

- **To be desirable.** Nature has wired us to want to be desirable to others. How else would we populate the planet? The need to feel desirable may drive us to look better (L'Oreal), smell good (Ban), or engage with others (Match.com).

- **To feel safe and secure.** Wanting to feel safe goes back to our primitive brain's desire to avoid pain or danger. This desire, of course, includes the need to keep our loved ones safe from harm as well. Companies like Volvo, Johnson & Johnson, and ADT are well aware of this urge. Who can forget the adorable baby protected by Michelin tires because "so much is riding on it"?

- **To feel significant.** Just like your employees who want a sense of purpose along with their coffee mug and computer, consumers want to feel as though they are doing or buying something worthwhile. This includes caring for others (Make-a-Wish Foundation), being of service (U.S. Army), or taking care of the planet (Simple Green).

Until just this past decade, companies relied on quantitative and qualitative research like consumer surveys and focus testing to get feedback on the effectiveness of advertising and marketing campaigns. The problem with this approach was that most people don't buy based on logic—they buy based on emotion, and our emotions are often well hidden from our conscious minds. It's only been since the advent of powerful magnetic imaging equipment, like the functional magnetic resonance imaging (fMRI) machines, that researchers have begun to peek inside our brains to get more accurate data on why we buy what we buy. Not that people were necessarily lying when they answered retail surveys, but they often didn't understand the path of tiny emotional reactions and mini-decisions that resulted in their habits. Enter the new science of *neuromarketing*.

Martin Lindstrom is the author of *Buyology: Truth and Lies About Why We Buy* and a guru of global branding. An expert at the forefront of neuromarketing, he has spent years studying the data resulting from some of the world's most comprehensive neuroscience studies on brand messages. Among his startling findings is the discovery that warning signs on cigarette labels actually prompt people to want to smoke.[2]

Yes, those nasty skull and crossbones and other far more grisly graphics actually get smokers excited about the idea of smoking and feed their desire to continue their habit. Drawn from data collected in a laboratory in London based on thousands of subjects who participated in one of the largest neuromarketing tests of all time, the evidence was clear. When asked by a researcher whether the *smoking kills* warnings gave them concern about their habit, most respondents answered yes. But when their brains were asked the same question via the MRI scans, they definitively answered no—exactly the opposite of what their conscious minds thought.

That is, when cigarette warnings were flashed before their eyes (even the especially gruesome ones displaying diseased lungs and open mouth sores that are featured on some packs overseas), an area of the brain called the nucleus accumbens, or "the craving spot," was stimulated, indicating their desire for the product. So what's stronger, our logical or our emotional brain? Well, across the globe, 10 million cigarettes are sold each minute, 1.4 billion people regularly use tobacco, and that number is expected to increase to 1.6 billion by 2025, despite millions of dollars spent on advertising and warning labels on cigarette packages in 123 countries. Think the tobacco industry knows a thing or two about branding? To say they are "killer marketers" is no exaggeration.

JOIN THE CLUB

If you've ever seen a group of smokers congregating outside the office high-rise, shunned by some but welcomed with open arms and cigarette packs by fellow smokers, you've seen an example of how brands bond people with similar habits, tastes, and aspirations. We gravitate toward those brands that engender a sense of comfort, familiarity, and dependability.

As social creatures, we naturally want to be part of the club— and not just any club, but the club that makes a statement about who we are as human beings. Many of us have already organized our lives around one or more "clubs," including church, school, community, or sports teams, as well as more literal clubs like Rotary, Toastmaster's, or your book club.

Just think about the coffee loyalists in your life. Whether you're a Peet's, Starbucks, or Dunkin' Donuts fan—or, like me, eschew those brands altogether in favor of independent neighborhood cafes— chances are this choice is less about the flavor of the coffee and more about which club gives you an authentic sense of belonging.

We react to brands very much like we react to people, deepening trust and loyalty over time. We have expectations for brands, on which skillful marketers build to evoke positive emotions. Ask a group of people what Volvo and BMW stand for, and most will say "safety" for the former and "high performance" for the latter. That's not a matter of chance but a carefully crafted message. Target and Tiffany both sell jewelry, but they appeal to two very different clubs, although Target has recently added a layer of discount sophistication with its low-cost designer goods that also appeal to people who could well afford Tiffany.

When Marcy tossed the soaps, she was refusing to be part of a club that didn't take aesthetics seriously. In that instance, the packaging alone sent a signal about the kind of club she was being invited to join.

But even beyond our initial reactions, brands must hold up to further scrutiny to gain our long-term loyalty, as was the case with my client Michael. After struggling with his weight for many years, Michael decided to try a weight loss regimen based on meal replacement shakes. Where other diets had failed, either because of their restrictiveness or inability to satisfy his hunger, this one worked. Over a period of several months, he lost 60 pounds and has kept it off since.

Intrigued with the shake product as well as the business model behind it, Michael explored becoming a distributor for the weight loss line, which was sold through direct marketing similar to Mary Kay Cosmetics or Herbalife. But once he explored the business end, he found that he disliked the vibe of the company as much as he liked the shakes. The management team was made up of young, aggressive entrepreneurs who were hell-bent on hard selling. They'd chosen a not-so-young but equally aggressive professional athlete as their spokesperson, whose sole purpose seemed to be yelling at people about their weight, their sales records, or both. The vibe of the group was such a bad fit for Michael's more intellectual sensibilities that not only did he choose not to pursue a distributorship with the company, but he actually switched to another shake product whose company image more closely fit his style. Groucho Marx may have said he didn't want to join any club that would have him as a member, but that's precisely what most of us want: to find a club that makes us instinctively feel like part of a closely connected community.

This is not to say that companies should attempt to be all things to all people. Quite the contrary. Disqualifying people who are not your core customers is a smart strategy. After all, why would you spend time investing in the wrong audience? If someone comes to my website looking for a financial strategist, rather than a branding strategist, I want him to go away as quickly as possible. Why waste either of our time? I don't want to spend my energy, or that of my team, chatting or sending materials or proposals to a non-prospect.

That's why, as counterintuitive as it may seem, a narrowly defined brand will always attract more people—more of the right people, that is. You need to spend your time interacting with your ideal club members, those whom author Seth Godin refers to as your "tribe,"[3] while the people who are not suitable for you—as customers, employees, or stakeholders—should go find the club that is right for them. If you can refer those wrong prospects on to someone who's a good fit, even better. Win-win.

DISCOVERING YOUR EMOTIONAL ASSIGNMENT

I'm sure it won't come as any big surprise that the first step in creating a successful brand is to become very clear about the value you provide. I mean *really* clear, focused, and committed. Once you are committed to functioning at the highest level of self and you're crystal clear about your value proposition, you're ready to embark on an undertaking without which your professional life would remain unfulfilled and your personal life incomplete—you've discovered your *emotional assignment.* Let me give you an example.

It's somewhat ironic that an online auto business was created on a commuter train, but that's how it happened for Web2Carz.com. Co-founders Alex Bravy and Ben Wallach took the same commuter train back and forth to work each day from the suburbs of Highland Park into the city of Chicago. At the time, Wallach was employed at travel company Orbitz.com, and Bravy was working at online job search site Monster.com. As they chatted each day on their 45-minute ride, they discovered a shared passion for cars, technology, and the possibility of launching their own business. Soon their conversation turned into collaboration, and they began to focus on how to pool their talents and resources to create an online start-up company.

Both had strong skills in technology and high-traffic websites, and Wallach also had specific expertise in the online auto industry, having worked at Cars.com. After talking through numerous business ideas, they zeroed in on a web-based automobile site that would help shoppers research different car models, apply for a loan, locate a car, and contact the seller. While Wallach focused on business operations, Bravy took on the technology, and both weighed in on strategic direction.

Grabbing their favorite workspace on the commuter train's second floor—which they jokingly referred to as "the office"— whenever they could, Wallach and Bravy began working through the basics. Bravy used his commute time to prospect for clients and build business relationships, while Wallach worked on the design and architecture of the website. Since both had families and mortgages, they were determined not to leave their day jobs until they had proof of concept and a solid revenue model.

Working diligently step-by-step while continuing to fulfill the obligations of their current jobs, the pair tackled one issue at a time. At one point, they discovered their advertising program wasn't giving them the financial return they expected. After tossing around some potential solutions during their afternoon commute, they chose a new course of action. Wallach made the fix while still on the train, and by the time they got home, they could already see things turning around. As Bravy says, "It's amazing the era that we live in. Not only can you see the results of your work almost instantly during the course of one train ride, but also by the time you get home, your whole world can change from being negative to positive."[4] In this case, both literally and financially.

Working during commutes, plus nights and weekends for more than a year, the two created the foundation for Web2Carz. They soon quit their jobs to go full-time, incorporating in 2007 when others in the auto industry were looking for bailouts or hunkering down and waiting for the recession to pass. It turned out to be a good bet. Web2Carz now has twelve employees and in 2011 was named on the Inc. 5000 List of America's Fastest Growing Private Companies, with a three-year sales growth of 641 percent. The company continues to evolve and recently announced the addition of a digital publishing arm and online magazine featuring daily original content about cars and technology. They brought on respected journalists and auto experts from the Associated Press, *mph* magazine, High Gear Media, and other industry publications to test drive cars, write reviews, and provide content on autos as well as travel, food, music, and lifestyle. As Bravy says, "We're giving our readers everything they need to know about buying a new car and the auto lifestyle."

CAPTURE THE MINDSHARE SNAPSHOT: NAMING OF AN ICON

In every chapter, I want to give you a quick "CTM" snapshot, a sort of mini-Mindshare, of an individual or organization that illustrates a specific example of the concept we're exploring within the chapter. These brief case studies on branding, drawn from my own clients and colleagues, will illustrate a business *Challenge* and then offer some strategic *Tactics* used to solve the problem. For *More* information as well as tips, tools, and resources regarding the challenge presented in the CTM snapshot, you can visit www.LibbyGill.com.

NAMING OF AN ICON

Marc Hershon, creative director at branding company Lexicon, which specializes in naming, has been involved in the naming of countless products and services, including the Apple PowerBook, Intel's Pentium Chip, Dasani Water, and, my personal favorite, the Swiffer.

The naming process at Lexicon starts with a client meeting that determines what the product or service is intended to do and for whom it does what it does. This meeting is followed by a free-form brainstorming session in which every idea is captured and put into a giant mind map. The list is distilled down and checked for legal clearance and URL availability, and then the names are vetted in more than 70 countries to ensure that the words don't have a meaning that might be objectionable in another language. A classic example of this mistake is the Chevy Nova—"*no va*" means "doesn't go" in Spanish. When Hershon and the Lexicon team were presented with a cutting-edge telephonic product by a group of young engineers from Waterloo, Canada, they had no idea how iconic the name they chose would become.[5]

CHALLENGE

The team at Research in Motion (RIM) invented a new version of a phone pager that could carry two lines of text—a revolutionary invention at the time—and they needed a name for it. RIM wanted to reach a business rather than consumer market, but since they themselves were hardly a household name like tech giants IBM and Hewlett-Packard, they recognized that the product name would be critical to their marketing and sales efforts.

TACTICS

After considering a number of names, including the early favorite PocketLink, which described what the product did—namely, linked you to your office via a device you could carry in your pocket—Lexicon decided to go in an entirely different direction. Recognizing that executives, the intended market, might be understandably hesitant to embrace a device that would keep them tethered to the office, the Lexicon team decided that the name should be innocuous, even friendly. Hence, the BlackBerry. Interestingly, most of the RIM folks were unfamiliar with the non-native fruit, but they liked the offbeat name because they thought it would stand out among technology products. It wasn't long before the name became so synonymous with the businessperson's addictive need to connect with the office that it was dubbed the "CrackBerry." A left-handed compliment, perhaps, but definitely a sign that the BlackBerry had captured the mindshare of popular culture. In the ultimate naming compliment, in January 2013, RIM changed the company's name to Blackberry.

MORE

Although brands and brand names sometimes run their course, Hershon cautions that it's vital to stay vigilant about protecting your brand name. Otherwise you run the risk of your brand becoming genericized, like the Escalator or Aspirin, both brand names at one time. To learn more about protecting your brand name, go to the Capture the Mindshare section on www.LibbyGill.com.

Once you're clear on your *emotional assignment*, it's time to start building your brand and business—all it takes is the decision to *Commit*. In Chapter Two, we'll look at some companies whose unflagging commitment to excellence has helped them succeed despite internal hardships, external challenges, and economic uncertainty. Then you can begin to put these Mindshare Methods into action.

Chapter Two

COMMIT

The Non-Negotiable Promise of Excellence

We are what we repeatedly do. Excellence, then, is not an act but a habit.

—Aristotle

WHEN RUDY KARSAM, CEO OF GLOBAL HUMAN RESOURCES FIRM Kenexa, says that his company defines trust by making a promise and then fulfilling the commitment, he's ready to back it up. "We have a 90 percent renewal rate among our clients, we serve more than half of the Fortune 500, and we're operating in more than 100 countries," states Karsam in the welcome video posted on the company's website. But the stats don't begin to tell the story for this company that prides itself on making business personal. "Our business is so focused on relationships," continues Karsam, "that our people have been in our clients' wedding parties, they've become godparents to their children, and many have become lifelong friends."[1] If that's not making business personal, I don't know what is.

While that level of connection and commitment might not fit every company's business model, it has certainly worked wonders for Kenexa—and their clients. A worldwide leader in management and employee performance, or what they call "improving companies and enriching lives," Kenexa was founded in 1987 as an employee search firm. Through organic expansion as well as the strategic acquisition of more than 25 other companies, Kenexa grew from their roots in recruiting to include expertise in research, e-learning, technology, compensation, and leadership solutions. The company has been so successful, in fact, that it was purchased by IBM in 2012.

As I've said before, behaviors and decisions—including those that appear to be strictly business—are based as much, if not more, on emotion than on logic. Kenexa has built their brand on understanding the interrelationship between the emotional/personal and the rational/ business aspects of commerce and helping clients navigate those delicate dynamics at every level of the organization. In this chapter, we'll see why commitment to excellence is part of the DNA of the most successful companies, Kenexa included, and how you can adopt some of their best practices to unfailingly fulfill your brand promise.

As Kenexa grew, they realized that they needed to put their own organization under the cultural microscope in order to refine their internal brand message for the benefit of their employees. At the same time, they wanted to enhance their external brand in order to recruit and retain people who would be passionate about the company and the work they were doing. Interestingly, the past work of early twentieth-century Swiss psychiatrist Dr. Carl Jung on the theory of archetypes, or ancient images derived from what he termed the "collective unconscious," laid the foundation for Kenexa's reinvented future.

THE PEARSON ARCHETYPAL SYSTEM

In 2008, deepening their intellectual reach into the emotional and cultural aspects of the workplace, Kenexa acquired research conducted by Dr. Carol S. Pearson, then a professor of leadership studies at the University of Maryland. Using the work of Carl Jung and Joseph Campbell as a foundation, Dr. Pearson had created a conceptual thesis and a multi-faceted process based on well-known archetypes to help professionals discover their deepest motivations in both work and life.[2] Kenexa worked in partnership with Dr. Pearson to create their own *Cultural Branding Process*, an effort that included further developing an instrument she created, now called the Organizational and Team Culture Indicator (OTCI). This survey is a powerful tool that Kenexa uses with client companies for external employment branding, internal communications, and strategic leadership training.

The process is based on the belief that every company's culture and brand identity fall into 1 of 12 distinct archetypes based on familiar personalities from stories, myths, and legends. Similar to my concepts of leadership DNA and the inherent behavioral styles of leaders that I describe in my previous book, *You Unstuck: Mastering the New Rules of Risk-taking in Work and Life*, identifying ourselves as archetypes allows us to better understand how we operate individually and within a team structure.[3]

When we are able to recognize a company's dominant archetype, we have a window into the behavior, values, decision-making approach, and communication style of that company—a critical foundation for building an engaged workforce and an authentic brand with which to influence prospective clients and recruit future employees. This archetypal structure also helps us see why some employees are naturally a good "culture fit," while others—whose individual archetypes may run counter to the company's dominant one—may find it harder to assimilate into the organization.

Before we look at Kenexa's process (as well as some of their client outcomes in later chapters), take a look at Dr. Pearson's 12 archetypes listed below. Although the categories are based directly on her work (which you can find on her website at www.herowithin.com), I've added additional descriptions and examples to stimulate your thinking about where your organization fits into this framework. Even if you've never considered your company's style in storytelling terms, you will likely spot yourself in one or more of these scenarios. See if you recognize your own dominant and secondary archetypes, as well as those of your company, within these 12 types.

- **Innocent.** Optimistic, idealistic, and hopeful, the Innocent works diligently on the belief that everything will turn out all right in the end. Although they sometimes need to check their inclination to live in denial, Innocent organizations often blast through barriers that others cannot, thanks in part to a state of blissful ignorance. *Think Save the Children*, Forrest Gump, *or Trader Joe's.*

- **Everyperson.** Down-to-earth and empathetic, the Everyperson is a great team player and collaborator, although he has a tendency to turn into the victim or contribute to an Us vs. Them mentality when things don't go his way. *Think The Gap, Target, or Tom Hanks.*

- **Hero.** Born to fight injustice or overcome significant challenges, Heroes live to defy the odds and accomplish results. Heroes must be mindful not to consider others the enemy when they don't agree or rush through challenges without proper due diligence. *Think FedEx, Nelson Mandela, or Superman.*

- **Caregiver.** Compassionate and nurturing, the Caregiver lives to serve. Caregivers work with selfless dedication as advocates for others but must not succumb to martyrdom or workaholism. *Think APlaceforMom.com, Campbell's Soup, or Mother Teresa.*

- **Explorer.** Ever adventurous, the Explorer loves challenges and new ideas. Explorers can be very successful at staying on top of trends and leading the way, but they must commit to a course of action rather than constantly seeking new for new's sake. *Think REI, Richard Branson, or Luke Skywalker.*

- **Lover.** Relationship-builders and passionate admirers of beauty, Lovers look for quality of life both at work and at home. They love to win people over and build consensus, but they must be careful not to be snobbish or dramatic. *Think Victoria's Secret, Vera Wang, or Andrea Bocelli.*

- **Revolutionary.** Unconventional, provocative, and cutting-edge, Revolutionaries must have a cause to which they can commit. They love to fight the status quo and are very good at getting people and companies "unstuck," but they have to be mindful of being overly reckless. *Think James Dean, Henry Ford, or Apple.*

- **Creator.** Imaginative, expansive, and inventive, Creators are great empire builders and love seeing ideas come to fruition. Often ahead of the curve, Creators are great at bringing products and services to life but have to be careful about overloading themselves. *Think J.K. Rowling, Pixar, or Benjamin Franklin.*

- **Magician.** Visionary, inspiring, and highly intuitive, Magicians do well in times of chaos and change. Able to see possibilities where others don't, Magicians can turn companies and ideas around with their unique sense of confidence but must be careful not to abuse their power. *Think Dr. Martin Luther King Jr., Facebook, or Frank Gehry.*

- **Ruler.** Powerful, results-driven, and confident, Rulers love to take charge and make things happen, but they must be careful not to manipulate others or get bogged down in procedure. *Think American Express, Hillary Clinton, or IBM.*

- **Sage.** Knowledge-driven, intelligent, and truth-seeking, the Sage wants to use intellect to solve the world's problems but needs to avoid becoming dogmatic or disconnected from the real world. *Think Dr. Oz, Albert Einstein, or Regeneron Pharmaceuticals.*

- **Jester.** Witty, playful, and spontaneous, the Jester usually solves problems and builds relationships through humor. Great at pulling teams together, the Jester can diffuse tension to bring the best out of people during stressful situations, but she must use caution not to seem overly childish. *Think Adam Sandler, Geico, or Taco Bell.*

Building on the core concept that every company's cultural identity falls within 1 of these 12 archetypes, Kenexa, through their tools, surveys, and expert guidance, helps their clients identify their archetype (or archetypes) and build upon that knowledge. Since my own work with executive and entrepreneurial branding is so much in alignment with Kenexa's philosophies, they were kind enough to share some of their branding success stories with me—many of which they've never shared publicly—starting with their own story.

KENEXA AND THE HERO CULTURE

After more than 20 years of rapid growth, Kenexa decided it was time to turn their expertise on themselves and submit to their proprietary Cultural Branding Process, comprising four action phases: Discover, Distill, Deliver, and Deploy. As Kenexa Chief Marketing Officer Tim Geisert told me, "We've been growing by leaps and bounds and have more than doubled [in size] since I've been here. And when that happens, many companies fall apart when it comes to the cultural pillars, so we wanted to find out what made us who we are. The whole archetype aspect shows you when you're at your best and also when you're at your worst. You don't really want to change who you are, but there's the dark side to an archetype and there's the upside to an archetype."[4]

The Kenexa team started with the preliminary Discover phase—which included reviewing existing data such as annual reports, press announcements, employee handbooks, and engagement surveys—just as they would with any other company. Next, they conducted open-ended interviews with executives, top employees, and outside experts to explore the culture from multiple perspectives to get a 360° view of the organization. In the last step of the Discover process, they took their own OTCI survey to determine the mix of archetypes, as well as the prevailing style, within Kenexa.

Perhaps not surprisingly, given their innovative problem-solving inclination, Kenexa leaders ranked highest in the Hero, Explorer, and Jester categories. While the Jester archetype might seem a bit of a surprise, as you'll see, this orientation is a core component of their culture. When the team interpreted the results, they concluded that the company "strive[s] to be the best in everything they do, easily overcoming challenges, consistently seeking opportunity and having fun while they do it." These findings confirmed many of the beliefs Kenexa's management already held about the company and seemed consistent with the company's history, as well as with Kenexa's vision for their future.

Following the Discover phase, Kenexa was ready to Distill the information into an internal and external foundation upon which the company could continue to build. This included synthesizing the rational facts (hard data), the emotional truths (soft data) and the company's personality (dominant archetype) into a brand story that would resonate with employees inside the company while increasing the awareness of clients outside Kenexa.

With the brand essence more clearly defined, it was time to initiate the Deliver phase, putting concepts into action. A cultural analysis and roster of recommendations was created for the company based on their Hero, Explorer, and Jester archetypes. According to Dr. Pearson's research, Hero organizations love to overcome challenges, defeat their adversaries, and achieve their goals. They are likely to embrace and admire colleagues who are "energetic, confident, tough-minded, competitive, aggressive, and consistently produce results."[5]

In addition to the Hero persona that dominates their culture, the Kenexa team also has a strong orientation toward the Jester, who loves laughter and playful interaction even—or especially—in the face of hard work and stress. And, finally, the company's Explorer side demonstrates an adventurous streak and a passion for seeking a better world. No wonder the Kenexa team chose Indiana Jones as a symbol for their culture and internal brand.

Based on the findings about their Hero culture, the company continued the Deliver process, creating materials that would define the brand and remind the Kenexa team about their commitment to deliver on their promises. They created a snapshot of the culture that they dubbed the 10Exa (rhymes with Kenexa), which was designed to help shape internal and external messaging and accurately reinforce the brand. Notice how simple and non-corporate the language is, yet how well it reflects the idea of the Hero–Jester–Explorer culture. Kenexa's 10Exa includes the following tenets:

THE 10EXA: WHAT IT'S LIKE TO WORK AT KENEXA

1. If you don't have passion for the place, you'll fail.
2. "Extreme service" means busting your butt for the client. Every day.
3. We're addicted to momentum. Without it, we wither.
4. If it won't sell, don't do it.
5. You're allowed to laugh your way through a problem.
6. Opportunity exists here. Find it.
7. Take initiative. Period.
8. Making friends replaces our organizational hierarchy.
9. Integrity is more than a word. It's in our DNA.
10. Our calling is to enrich lives by what we do.

To be fair, detractors say that if you need a lot of direction and structure, Kenexa might not be a good place for you to work. But for those of us who thrive on solving real problems and helping make people's lives noticeably better without a lot of bureaucratese, it sounds pretty darn great, right?

In the final Deploy stage, the creative folks went to town finding lots of fun ways to disseminate the message throughout the organization. They put the 10Exa on posters, t-shirts, mugs—basically, anything you could print on. But, of course, it's not just distributing stuff that gets a message accepted inside and outside a company. Deployment includes a strategic communications rollout that makes sure that everyone gets the big brand picture, the science and research behind it, and, most important, understands the "Where do I fit in?" factor—a critical step in aligning the micro or personal brand with the macro or organizational brand.

When the brand essence is communicated badly, it can turn off a lot of people and lose a lot of momentum. When it's done well, it can transform your workforce into a powerhouse of employee engagement and your satisfied customers into gleeful brand evangelists, joyfully spreading the word about the great work that you do. Right now, let's take a look at how you build excellence into the total brand experience, what challenges you can expect to encounter, and how some smart companies have overcome them.

MINDSHARE MINUTE: EXCELLENCE AT WORK

Ask yourself the following questions and then go to www.LibbyGill.com for a Mindshare Minute tool that will help you define what *excellence at work* means in your organization.

- When you're operating at your best in the workplace, what does it look like? Name three to five actions that specifically epitomize that level of excellence.
- How do you systematize excellence, that is, what do you do to make it a habit?
- If you could only commit to one professional promise, what would it be?

THE EXPERIENCE OF TOTAL EXCELLENCE

The Internet has changed everything for the brick-and-mortar retailer. With the proliferation of online stores and daily deal sites, not to mention the ease of shopping from home in your jammies, who needs to go to the mall anymore? This shift has meant that retailers have had to reimagine what the shopping experience could feel like in reality.

Glimcher Realty Trust, an investment trust that specializes in developing shopping malls and lifestyle entertainment centers, admits that if shoppers can buy it online, they probably will.[6] Chairman Michael P. Glimcher notes that his core customer can buy her clothes online, but she can't get a salad or glass of wine with her girlfriends online. The relentless pursuit of that face-to-face experience prompted their company executives to try out new ideas from laser tag to yoga to blow-dry bars—anything that might bring shoppers back to their properties. And Glimcher isn't alone; malls across America have been slowly adding more service-oriented tenants to their retail mix. So if you've noticed more shoe repair shops and specialty cafes in your own local mall, that's no accident.

Glimcher's Arizona mall, Scottsdale Quarter, has about 50 percent clothing-only retailers, but the company has made sure that the rest of the mall tenants include plenty of lifestyle experiences or convenience services, preferably ones that can bring shoppers back once a week, like hairdressers or yoga studios. One of the stores that Glimcher brought in from New York City (where its headquarters and two retail outlets are located) is Make Meaning, a "creative destination" where kids and adults can create pottery, jewelry, candles, and other handicrafts. The big advantage of having a shop like Make Meaning in the mall is that visitors to the craft boutique often have to wait for their reservation or come back to pick up their fired pottery, leaving them free time to wander through the property.

Rick Caruso is the developer behind innovative shopping experiences such as the Grove in Los Angeles, which includes an open plaza where the entertainment TV series *Extra* is taped. Caruso noted in the *New York Times* that traditional malls were "intended to put the old Main Street out of business and divert that shopper. It's wonderfully ironic that that whole thing has come back around."[7] Ironic, yes, but also very intentional.

Still, it's a work in progress. Glimcher is making changes as they see what lends itself to the total experience approach. They dumped a Dollar Tree from a mall in Ohio, replacing it with an Ulta Beauty, a store that lets you sample cosmetics before you buy them. They booted a Benetton store in their Elizabeth, New Jersey mall and brought in a Lego store, complete with classes in Lego construction. Smart way to let a busy mom or dad sit down for a few minutes while the kids tinker happily! As Glimcher says, "It's retail Darwinism."[8] Even in the shopping mall, adaptability rules the day.

SENSORY BRANDING

Close your eyes for a moment and imagine your fondest reminiscences of home. Maybe they're memories of when you were a child. Perhaps they're fond memories of your parents' or grandparents' home. Zero in on what makes the memories so special. Does the unmistakable aroma of your mom's chocolate chip cookies baking come to mind? What about that warm, chewy texture when you bite into one fresh from the oven, prompting you to lick that last bit of chocolate off your fingertips? Or maybe you recall the scent of your grandmother's perfume or the sound of your grandfather listening to news on the radio. For some people, it's the smell of cedar or pine or fresh linen drying in the sun that triggers those happy memories. It could be the softness of a bed or the warmth of a comforter.

These experiences may all be very different, yet they have a common thread: They're related to your sensory perception—your sense of smell, sight, taste, touch, or sound.

Place those memories in the context of the science of the brain and suddenly they're not so magical, which is actually good news for your brand. Neuroscience research shows that smell, sound, sight, taste, and touch play a prominent role in creating emotional attachment and strongly affect how we create memories. That's why we may so strongly associate pleasant smells and tactile experiences with home or other connections. But that association also works in ways we don't expect, such as influencing our buying decisions.

When it comes to brand building, it literally pays to know a thing or two about how to involve the senses to evoke an emotional response in your customer and create an attachment to your brand. You may already be familiar with the cookie technique real estate agents use to build emotional attachment to houses they're trying to sell. By baking cookies or lighting vanilla-scented candles prior to showing a house, real estate agents re-create that homey feeling for prospective buyers.

Think about it. What would you rather buy: a cold, empty house devoid of furnishings or a home with a fire in the hearth and the scent of cookies wafting from the kitchen? Here's the kicker, though: You're not likely to get a bite. The scent is there to evoke a visceral response, unbeknownst to you, and leave you wanting more. The realtor wants you to create an emotional attachment to the house, not the chocolate chips.

MULTI-SENSORY MAKES GOOD SENSE

While some companies engage all the senses because it helps create brand recognition, others do it because engaging all the senses creates a richer, fuller experience. In fact, scientific research shows that sensory branding is most likely to work best when you engage multiple senses.[9] An example of this can be seen in the emergence of 6-D movie theaters, in which you not only watch a 3-D movie but also feel the seats move, feel air rush at you, and smell fragrance sent toward your nostrils by jets. You may not yet have experienced these things at your Cineplex, but you can also think about amusement park "motion rides" that engage all those senses.

This kind of experience is not that different from stepping into a Starbucks, where you get the carefully calculated multi-sensory rush of the familiar green logo (sight), the scent of coffee brewing (smell), the griiiind of coffee beans and background chit-chat (sound), the feel of the warm cup in your hand (touch), and, of course, the sip of your favorite caffeinated brew (taste). You are fully engaged—far more than you even realize—before you can say grande non-fat latte.

Trader Joe's grocery store chain is another example of the seamless way marketers can create that multi-sensory experience. Walk into a Trader Joe's and the first thing you'll see is a clever display of their sale items front and center, opening up to brightly lit aisles with homey wooden shelving. The welcoming fragrance of plants and flowers displayed near the front of the store greets your nose as you enter. Organic fruits and vegetables are also placed up front, which underscores the company's commitment to quality and healthful offerings. Food samples engage shoppers' taste sensations, and employees are allowed to open any product a shopper would like to taste.

But TJ's goes a step further to reinforce their brand's unique warmth and quirkiness. "Crew members," as they're called, wear Hawaiian shirts to go along with the island import style of the chain. Stores are locally themed—one of my favorites near LAX is '50s airport style, with kitschy propellers on the wall and numbered "runways" instead of checkout stands. You also hear the occasional ringing of bells, which is actually a clever means for employees to communicate instead of using a PA system that would disrupt the shopping experience. Here's what Trader Joe's says on their website about their bell system, in their typical tongue-in-cheek fashion: "It's a kind of Trader Joe's Morse code. Those blustery PA systems just didn't feel right to us, so we came up with a simple system to communicate—island style. One bell lets our Crew know when to open another register. Two bells mean there are additional questions that need to be answered at the checkout. Three bells call over a manager-type person. Honestly, it's much easier than the ole message in a bottle trick." Even the company's sales circular, dubbed the "Fearless Flyer" (more of TJ's cornball humor), is printed on inexpensive recyclable paper that adds to the overall brand promise of providing low-cost, high-quality goods from exotic locales.[10]

For a fun multi-sensory experiment, you can visit the Jelly Belly jellybean factory in Fairfield, California. The company offers tours of its manufacturing plant, where visitors can watch as brightly colored jellybeans tumble along conveyor belts and get sorted by bean-packing machines into gigantic bins. Well aware of the sensory interplay between smell and taste, guides offer the guests new flavors of jellybeans to sample but suggest that they hold their noses while doing so. Volunteers usually taste nothing, but once they unleash their sniffer, the taste becomes apparent—and the joke's on them. It's usually a "flavor" like baby wipes or earwax, which, of course, gets the hoped-for "Yeccch!" response from visitors.[11]

While the Jelly Belly folks get to reinforce their brand of sweet fun, they know that as you chew, you're forcing air through your nasal passages and sending smells right to your brain. Olfactory senses and their corresponding memories are generally stronger than other senses, including sight.[12] That's exactly why seeing a cozy home like the one in which you grew up may grab your attention, but it's the smell of the cookies baking inside that's the clincher when it comes to making you want to buy.

SIGHT WONDERFUL

Although smell may be the most powerful sense in terms of long-lasting memories, it's not exploitable for many brands. The visual or sight senses, however, are relevant to almost all businesses and should be expressed in a variety of ways. Here's a great example: in a matter of five short years, an unknown juice brand went from obscure to ubiquitous thanks to some smart marketing, eye-catching design, and provocative advertising.

In 2002, POM Wonderful released its distinctive curvy bottles and familiar POM heart-shaped logo, and sales rocketed. The package's round, double-globe bottle stands out on shelves, and the heart-shaped logo reinforces the company's bold heart-healthy claims. But it may be the unmistakable deep purple color—both a smart marketing move and a nod to the fruit itself—that has most solidified the POM Wonderful brand in consumers' minds.[13] Marketing by using color is a powerful but underestimated way to connect with customers. But can a simple color alone really drive sales? If you have any doubt, all you need to do is refer to the pale blue boxes wrapped with white ribbon that signify that the gift inside is an exquisite item from none other than Tiffany's. Tiffany's has used those boxes since 1837, and both the boxes and the color are now registered trademarks.

Color doesn't always indicate high-end luxury, of course. Sometimes it hits the bull's-eye, like Target's signature red and white logo. Or it might offer the promise of all-natural ingredients, like the soft yellow and red color palette of Burt's Bees. The natural lip balm and lotion company uses an illustrated likeness of Burt—who was actually one of the original co-founders of the brand—and drawings of bees. The packaging's homey graphics and warm colors create a down-home feel and artisanal style that evoke a sense of trustworthy comfort.

TASTEFUL BRANDING

Incorporating the sense of taste can be a bit tricky for brands, especially those that don't do live tasting events and can't offer product samples as a matter of practicality. But there are other clever ways companies can incorporate taste into their brand. In fact, creating taste experience is First Flavor's brand. The company produces flavor strips, much like the popular breath strips already on the market. The "peel and taste" flavor strips act as a way for customers to sample a product but also create a strong sensory impression that makes the taste of the brand memorable to the customer. Companies like Captain Morgan have promoted their key lime–flavored rum this way, V8 has marketed its new flavor of V-Fusion fruit and vegetable mixture in this way, and Arm & Hammer has given customers a taste of its whitening toothpaste by using First Flavor's innovative taste strips.[14]

Further exploiting trends in taste, some companies are finding ways to incorporate new favorites into their current product lines. In 2012, hot and spicy flavors became the "hottest" trend, according to the "Heat and Mapping Report" by market research publisher Packaged Facts and San Francisco–based strategic food and beverage agency CCD Innovation.[15] Slim Jim, maker of beef jerky and "meat sticks," jumped on board with a new flavor and customer challenge all in one with their Slim Jim® DARE. The product line includes three spicy flavors that range from Kinda Hot Chili Pepper to Freakin' Hot Jalapeno, topping out with Really Freakin' Hot Habanero.

Taco Bell is another company that took an existing product and upped the taste ante. In 2012, Taco Bell launched their Doritos Locos taco, partnering with Doritos to make the product's taco shells. In just ten weeks, 100 million had been sold, making it the most successful product launch in Taco Bell's 50-year history. The company has already announced plans to release a Doritos Cool Ranch–flavored taco.[16]

BRAND SCENTS

Taste doesn't happen without scent, but scent can certainly happen without taste. And marketers of non-edibles have learned to rely heavily on certain scents to woo consumers and sell products. Car companies such as Rolls Royce use spray scents to imprint their brands in the minds and memories of consumers. Rolls Royce even went so far as to reconstruct the scent of its classic 1965 Silver Cloud and now sprays it under the seats of their new cars.[17] In a great display of multi-sensory derring-do, in 2012, the company unveiled their Rolls-Royce Ghost Six Senses car at the Beijing Auto Show. The car features a unique scent processed into its interior materials, but it also appeals to other senses with its cool chrome, supple leather, deep pile lamb's wool rugs in the interior and trunk, and an amplified sound system. Not to leave out taste, passengers in the back seats can indulge in their favorite beverages courtesy of the chilled drink compartment.[18]

Of course, cars aren't the only items we buy for which scents have an effect on our buying habits. Many companies use fragrance to influence the shopping experience: Victoria's Secret uses potpourri in its stores, and Bloomingdale's uses different scents for different departments, such as lilac for lingerie and tanning lotion for the swimsuits. Taking this idea one step further, having a signature scent that isn't found anywhere else can be a distinct advantage in creating identity and brand specificity. Singapore Airlines invested in a trademark scent nearly 20 years ago that they use in the lobby, on pillows, and even on their flight attendants.[19]

Too much of a good thing can backfire, however, as Abercrombie & Fitch found out. Prompted by the strong—some say "gagging"—scent called "Fierce" that is sprayed heavily throughout the store at regular intervals, a group of adolescents in gas masks called Teens Turning Green staged a protest outside San Francisco's Westfield Mall, complaining about the toxic chemicals used in the store's cologne.

Sony Style, a chain of electronics stores, adopted their own subtle blend of vanilla and mandarin orange fragrance to relax shoppers and make their electronics less intimidating, particularly to women.[20] And in what may be the most grandiose scent branding I've yet seen, the award-winning Broadmoor Resort in Colorado Springs pipes its signature scent, "Optimism," throughout the premises, both indoors and out. As the Broadmoor claims, the scent is "produced from the essential oils of lemongrass and sage, whose notes are meant to be both uplifting and soothing."[21]

SEE ME, FEEL ME, TOUCH ME

The feeling of an object's texture, heft, and shape has a lot to do with whether a customer will buy it or not. Who hasn't fondled those neatly folded t-shirts or sweaters in the front of a Gap store—cleverly poised on a round table right at hand height—wondering if you're ruining some sales kid's day now that everything has to be refolded? Quite the opposite—that's exactly what they want you to do. Touching is one step closer to buying.

According to Dr. John A. Bargh of Yale, along with MIT researcher Dr. Joshua M. Ackerman and Harvard graduate student Christopher C. Nocera, textures, shapes, and weights can influence decisions.[22] Their study, involving six experiments and hundreds of people, demonstrated how touch and texture affect the way people behave. The scientists discovered that people sitting on hard, cushionless chairs are less likely to compromise in price negotiations than their soft chair–sitting counterparts. They also found that interviewers holding heavy clipboards are likely to be taken more seriously by job applicants than those with lighter clipboards. How does that apply to marketing your products or services? Knowing how to incorporate the touch sense into even the smallest nuances of your business can influence how your customers perceive your brand. Everything from the kind of carpet in an office to the finishes of desktops and counters and the fabric of the curtains on the windows can create a tactile experience and thus an emotional imprint. Objects like coffee cups and pens can also affect perception. Typically, people equate quality with the heft of an object. Therefore, holding a heavy, smooth pen when signing contracts will give a much different impression than holding a cheap ballpoint pen.

Shape, in addition to texture, can have a powerful effect on brand recognition, especially for tactile products. Coca-Cola bottles were a hit in part because of their curve, which gives them a pleasant grip but also conjures up a smooth, flowing feeling that creates an identity. Toblerone packages its chocolate bars in a distinctive triangular box that is connected with the brand in consumers' minds.

MINDSHARE MINUTE: BRANDED BUSINESS CARD

Go to www.LibbyGill.com and take the Branded Business Card test to see what the shape, weight, texture, and color of your card says about your company.

SOUND DECISIONS

Let's not forget how sound plays into our buying decisions. If the sound of a cash register is music to your ears, then you better be pumping out the right sounds to the ears of your customers— from your hold music on your phone to the sound track in your store. Sound is a powerful tool in creating brand awareness as well as influencing your customer's buying decisions. J. C. Penney (as well as other department stores) has been known to use a system that plays certain types of music at certain times of the day. Their stores also play music by demographics; for instance, stores in locations with a bigger Hispanic population will play more Latin music. Victoria's Secret plays classical music for a more upscale image, while Abercrombie & Fitch appeals to its youthful customer base with upbeat and loud music.

Sound can also be relatable to a specific brand, in much the same way smell and touch can. If you heard the giggle of the Pillsbury Doughboy, it would probably instantly conjure up an image of that iconic character. That giggle has been used in Pillsbury's branding for so many years that it has become indelibly linked to the character and brand. Microsoft's startup sound for its Windows operating system and Yahoo's three-note yodel are also closely related to those brands. NBC was a pioneer in identifying how closely linked sound could be to their brand when they became the first company to register a sound trademark in 1950 for their three-note G–E–C played on chimes.

Even the Olympics' unmistakable Da-Da-Da-Da-Da-Da sound is protected. (Bet you could hear that in your head, right?) Brand identification is so important that everything surrounding the Olympics brand—the sound, rings, motto, and logo—are all trademarked and vigilantly policed for infringement. Sponsors of the Olympics pay big bucks to gain rights to those symbols, so they expect a level of protection for the investment, and rightfully so.

CAPTURE THE MINDSHARE SNAPSHOT: THE MONIMETER

When my client, noted fitness expert Monica Nelson, who trains such celebrities as Cheryl Tiegs and Mia Sara (and me), wanted to expand her brand to include both her private fitness training and her healthy recipes, it was time for a brand overhaul. Instead of combining these two different, but obviously related, areas, we decided to develop an entirely new brand and website for her vast library of "healthy comfort food" recipes.

Moni, as she is called by friends and clients, has built her reputation as a private chef and food blogger on her belief that as long as we eat nutritious food most of the time, we are not only entitled but obligated to have the occasional treat day, since it keeps us from feeling deprived. She may be the only fitness trainer, in fact, who actually bakes homemade cookies for her clients. If you want to see how visuals can get your taste buds going, just take a peek at MoniMeals.com.[23]

CHALLENGE

We wanted to put a spotlight on Monica's brand positioning of eating foods that range from healthy to decadent while showcasing her more than 300 recipes. And we also wanted to provide some way for recipe users to get a quick snapshot of the healthfulness (or not) of each recipe without having to deliver details about calorie count, sodium, fiber, and so on.

TACTICS

Since Moni is a chef and fitness trainer—and not a nutritionist—she didn't even want to begin to put herself in the position of advising people on heart-healthy foods or immune-building diets. It wasn't appropriate, and it just wasn't her thing.

But we did want to have some fun with the idea that you could eat healthy and still enjoy your treats. So we came up with the MoniMeter, a fun visual icon that immediately shows you a range of recipes from foods that are "Deliciously Healthy" all the way up to those that are "Decadently Indulgent." It's a bit like the little thermometer on the salsa jar that shows you the heat scale from mild to spicy. We used the great online tool 99Designs.com to run a contest calling for designers to create a graphic icon that would be playful but also instructive about the recipe contents.

MORE

Go to www.LibbyGill.com to find my favorite recipes from MoniMeals.com—all rated on the MoniMeter for health and/or decadence.

Now that you've thought through the brand commitment you're making to your customers and clients, let's move on to how *Collaboration* plays a vital part in your branding efforts.

Chapter Three

COLLABORATE

Creating Your Brand One Conversation at a Time

If two men on the same job agree all the time, then one is useless. If they disagree all the time, both are useless.

—Darryl F. Zanuck

LOCATED IN THE HEART OF THE SOUTHWEST, FARMINGTON, NEW MEXICO sits in the shadow of the San Juan Mountains near the convergence of the Animas, La Plata, and San Juan Rivers. Called *Totah* in Najavo, meaning "Three rivers," the town is a rich blend of Native American culture, tranquil desert landscapes, and world-class outdoor activities such as skiing and hiking.

It also happens to be the home of one of the best examples of collaboration I've ever seen in business: the San Juan Regional Medical Center (SJRMC). The spirit of collaboration runs so deep in the SJRMC's corporate culture that you can actually hear it in their brand language. Their conversations and even their website are so rich in reverence for human beings and their inherent value that the medical center seems to have as much relationship to the spiritual world as it does the scientific. In point of fact, both are important to them.

Defining and delivering upon their authentic value is so fundamental to the SJRMC that, according to Vice President of Marketing Catherine Zaharko, they spent an entire year just to get the language right. While in some organizations this might have resulted in losing sight of the forest for all the trees, at San Juan, the case was exactly the opposite. By focusing deeply and specifically on creating a unique brand language, they created an unshakeable foundation that truly captured what was most important to them. Take a look at the SJRMC's listing of their core values, which focuses as much on personal development as it does on physical wellness:

- **Sacred Trust.** Everyone who works at the hospital, in any capacity, is considered to have entered into a covenant with the patients, patient families, and each other to "do the right thing no matter what." Now there's a clear commitment to excellence.

- **Personal Reverence.** This value states that each person— whether patient, family, friend, or staff member—must be treated as a unique and valued being. As a result, tolerance and respect are elevated to a level of "reverence." According to the center's code, healing implies a connection not only between caregiver and patient or art and science, but also between head and heart. That's as good a definition of "capturing the mindshare" as I've ever heard.

- **Thoughtful Anticipation.** The SJRMC thinks of preparation as part of their commitment to excellence. They are continually involved in the process of innovation and problem solution, as well as learning from everything they do and have done in the past.

- **Team Accountability.** This is the crux of the SJRMC's sense of stewardship and obligation to patients, employees, and community, as they believe that teamwork and quality are inextricably linked.

- **Creative Vitality.** More than mere awareness that needs will change and best practices will evolve, the principle of creative vitality calls for a blend of enthusiastic exploration and rigorous science to answer not only the *how* questions but also the *why* questions.

"It took us a whole year to come up with those five values and their definitions. And then we spent another year working on how we would hardwire them into our organization," states Zaharko.

Now the values are put to daily use in matters ranging from patient care to housekeeping. Adds Beth Volkerding, San Juan's director of workforce excellence, "The values were put together to help us make decisions. For example, sacred trust is doing the right thing for the patient—no matter what. We also developed service standards, so if there's a conflict in the value piece, our service standards are like a decision tree. Our service standards are stewardship, efficiency, courtesy, and safety. And you work from the bottom up. So, we would sacrifice money first. We would sacrifice being efficient second. And if we had to sacrifice being courteous, we could, but we never sacrifice safety."[1]

While it's not unusual to hear hospitals and care providers talk about values and service, San Juan has something deeper at its core, which is manifested in some very unusual ways. Named a Top 100 Hospital of Choice by the American Alliance of Healthcare Providers, as well as Soliant Health's Sixth Most Beautiful Hospital in the United States, the SJRMC recognizes that the physical environment plays a significant role in the hospital's culture. So when faced with the need for expansion, it wasn't surprising that San Juan reached out to another innovative organization to help them blend multiple cultures into a workplace that could serve the needs of its patients and staff.

Because the medical center serves not just the Four Corners area of New Mexico where it is located but an entire region, hospital personnel interact with a wide and culturally diverse population. Among this population are members of the Navajo tribe, many of whom live in such remote regions that they may have never set foot inside a hospital before an illness—theirs or a loved one's—brings them to the SJRMC. Another group populating the region is made up of Christians, mostly Caucasian or Hispanic, who are as steeped in their traditions as the Navajo are in theirs. Balancing the needs, beliefs, and social systems of these two very different cultures—both represented in the workforce and among the patients—is a constant juggling act.

Since the SJRMC's core value of Sacred Trust states that "no one here should ever feel unconnected or alone," one of the issues of greatest concern to the staff had to do with the Navajo traditions surrounding death. According to the Navajos' belief, when a member of the tribe dies, the spirit of the departed passes out of the body with the last breath. If the spirit—including its most negative traits—has no physical route by which to escape, it will attach itself to someone present. Since there was no exit for trapped spirits within the hospital rooms at San Juan, the Navajo patients preferred to die alone, often with family members and staff waiting down the hall. While the families were accepting of the tradition, the hospital staff found it very difficult not to minister to the needs of their patients in their final hours. But the limitations of the hospital's physical layout, along with the patients' dying wishes, left them few options—that is, until the hospital brought in an award-winning design team with whom they could collaborate until they reached a successful, if challenging, outcome.[2]

Once you begin to expand your mindset to see that collaboration is far more than mere teamwork (although that's certainly part of it), you can take a more proactive approach to building a culture of collaboration. Let's look at some creative ways you can weave collaboration into your workplace.

COOPERATION ON STEROIDS

Ask ten managers what collaboration means at their company, and you're likely to get ten different answers. Some corporations, such as Disney, are experts at imposing a top-down approach, which results in driving brands—and revenues—through multiple areas of the company. That's why you're likely to continue to see the exploitation of great characters like *Toy Story* stars Woody and Buzz not only in films but also in theme parks and on cruise ships, toys, games, bedding, toothbrushes, and plenty of other objects by which the company can maximize its intellectual properties.

Apple Computers, known for Steve Jobs' famously combative form of collaboration, enforced teamwork by giving the company one bottom line. Jobs felt so strongly about having teams work with, and not against, each other that he established the shared balance sheet so that no individual division would put its agenda before that of the company.[3]

Perhaps the best definition of collaboration comes from Randy Nelson, former dean of Pixar University and now with DreamWorks. Nelson has said, "Collaboration is cooperation on steroids," meaning that collaboration is far more than just playing nicely together. It's an active dialogue, a constant back-and-forth interaction that requires everyone to put ideas forward and others to take those ideas and make something new from them, rather than just accepting them passively at face value. According to Nelson, one of Pixar's favorite means of collaboration is improvisation, much like you might see at a comedy club or on TV, which also happens to be one of my favorite techniques to use in communication training sessions with corporations.[4]

The cardinal rule of improv is simple: if a scene partner offers you something, whether it's an idea or an imaginary artichoke, it cannot be ignored or rejected. It's the "yes, and" versus the "no, but" approach, in which you take the offered idea and build on it, making your partner look good in the process. And isn't that what happens in the most productive meetings?

BRAND BUILDING BLOCK #2: TEN TECHNIQUES FOR CREATING A MORE COLLABORATIVE CULTURE

When I was first hired as head of media relations and corporate communications for Universal's worldwide television group, the company was undergoing a major transition. Despite (or perhaps because of) a long and stable history, at that time, many employees were entrenched in separate silos with relationships and reporting structures that had more to do with history than with logic.

It wasn't easy establishing rapport, let alone collaboration, with people who weren't sure they even wanted to know you. When I arrived, I decided to set up face-to-face meetings—lots of them. I had my assistant set up a series of 15-minute meetings with anyone who had any affiliation with the TV Group. I got in my golf cart, the best way to traverse the nearly 500-acre backlot, and I went on a campaign to introduce myself to anyone I thought I should get to know. I met with producers, costumers, researchers, accountants, tour guides—anyone who had any dealings with the studio's television unit. And when people saw that I had taken the time and trouble to get to know them—on their turf—it was the beginning of a working relationship.

Although there are many ways to go about inspiring, encouraging, charming, or improvising your way through collaboration, the following are some of my favorite techniques for creating an engaged and collaborative team.

1. **Share information appropriately.** Information is the organizational lifeblood of the decisions made in every company. Except for confidential or proprietary data that

can't be shared, pass information readily both up and down the pipeline that can help others make timely decisions. This doesn't mean just the facts but also the nuances of soft data (remember Kenexa's "emotional truths"), which can be critical. Although I've witnessed a few "over-sharers" among my executive coaching clients, I've seen far more people abuse their power by withholding information that would be useful to others, including their direct reports. Imagine the opportunities for collaboration you might be missing if you keep information to yourself.

2. **Establish high standards for communication.** Set the tone for the highest levels of communication, which are characterized by openness, transparency, and trust. Don't indulge in badmouthing or finger-pointing—they are non-productive time-wasters. Yes, people are human, and you can't eliminate all bad behaviors, but you can let it be known that respect for others is not only expected but demanded.

3. **Don't confuse collaboration with consensus.** Just because you've encouraged open collaboration doesn't mean that you should abdicate leadership or authority. There's still a chain of command and decisions to be made. Assuming you've got a management structure that makes sense, stick to it. People want to be led.

4. **Expect—and invite—conflict.** Encouraging collaboration means that you are also inviting conflict—that is, if you are the least bit authentic in your interactions. If you only stick to your inner circle to discuss challenges or brainstorm possibilities, you are likely to get answers similar to the ones you've come up with in the past. But

by broadening the collaborative circle and inviting opinions from people who might offer dissenting views or new information, you may open yourself up to more conflict, but you're also more likely to enterprise new solutions.

5. **Set ground rules and enforce them**. It's hard to play by the rules when you don't know what they are. But if you want to create a more collaborative culture in your organization, decide what's fair and off-limits and communicate both clearly. Be respectful of race, gender, culture, age, disabilities, sexual orientation, and any other sensitivity that goes with the multi-faceted workplace, but don't let the political correctness police rob you of humor or authenticity.

6. **Balance structure with flexibility.** The larger the organization, the more likely it is to have some kind of hierarchical structure in place. But that doesn't mean you should throw out flexibility or faith in others' good judgment. When I spoke at a leadership conference with former Southwest Airlines president Colleen Barrett, she said that Southwest's famous customer service policy could only exist because management trusted their employees to have better judgment in specific situations than any employee handbook could possibly mandate. In other words, hire good people, train them well, and get out of their way.

7. **Manage collaboration with the proper tools**. Once you've opened the pipeline of rigorous conversation and learned to navigate conflict, you'll want to capture all the great insights you're having. Put the proper tools in place, or you'll risk losing all that great brainpower. Try customer relationship software, project management programs, or whatever captures your ideas and helps transform

them into action. Even in a small business, systems like Salesforce.com or Zoho.com can ensure that your ideas stay organized and flowing.

8. **Insights require actions**. Collaboration is not an end in itself, but rather a means to an end. And tools and systems (see number 7) can help you capture your brainstorms, but they don't translate them into results. That's up to you, and it goes hand-in-hand with your commitment to excellence. The best collaborations are always followed up with action, even if the action is more collaboration.

9. **Give your group a sense of identity.** When you know who you are and what you stand for, it's a lot easier to trust each other. And trust is, of course, a huge factor in collaboration. Think about your collective identity and what you all have in common, whether you're part of an ongoing team or a one-time task force. You may want to put some language to your shared cause, vision, or team, just like the Kenexa folks did with their Indiana Jones hero figure.

10. **Break down the silos.** If you're in a position of power, do whatever you can to break down silos institutionally. If you're not in a formal leadership position, find ways to open the door to other teams, groups, and divisions. Try Kenexa's 10Exa rule about friendship replacing hierarchy and start building silo-busting relationships.

MANAGING CONFLICT WITH COMMUNICATION

Opening the door to collaboration may also mean that at some point you will be opening the door to conflict as well. While long-standing rifts may require more intervention, most minor conflicts can be managed with some simple communication strategies. Although many people consider compromise the default solution in disagreements, conflict coach and professional mediator Patti Cotton makes an important distinction between collaboration and compromise.[5] As Cotton explains it, "Compromise is when you concede something that is important to you to the other side, but you risk feeling resentful about it later. Collaboration is when you concede, but feel good about the decision." Cotton uses some of the following resolution techniques regularly in her practice.

THE YOU-I-WE APPROACH

When disagreements arise, take the conversation from "you" to "I" to "we" by acknowledging feelings. Most conflicts start with accusations such as, "You're always late" (a "you" statement). Rather than escalate the "and you always do..." dialogue, shift to an "I" statement that acknowledges feelings and emotions, such as "I can hear how frustrated you are." Elaborate, if necessary: "I haven't shared the health problems I've been having, and I really should have filled you in before now." Next, move to a more collaborative "we" question or statement, such as "Can we sit down together and talk about this? Maybe we can shift our morning meeting to make it work better for both of us." This way, while you're not necessarily rejecting or owning up to the problem, you can move to resolve it together.

THIRD GOOD OPTION

This is a great technique when either side gets so entrenched in a position that he or she can't see any other alternatives. In short, when *you* want this and *I* want that, you might pose the question: "Can we think about a third good option?" This defuses the situation and gets you both out of the I-versus-you mentality and onto neutral ground where resolution can happen.

THE FOUR DS

This strategy is from Roger Fisher of the Harvard Negotiation Project. It's especially useful when you don't have authority over a person or project but need to influence the situation. Rather than imposing your will, try asking the four D questions of Data, Diagnosis, Direction, and Do Next. They can get people off the dime and into decision-making mode more quickly than a combative back and forth:

- Data—What is the problem?
- Diagnosis—What are the possible causes?
- Direction—What strategies should we consider?
- Do Next—What do we want to do next?

Now that we've looked at some ways to increase collaboration by building trust, transparency, and respect, let's take a look at the collaboration-based company that the SJRMC brought in to help design the hospital expansion.

THE BRAND EXPERIENCE

When the team at the SJRMC turned to award-winning experiential design firm Kahler Slater, they were looking for more than a new hospital wing. They were looking for a bridge between cultures. Kahler Slater was a perfect choice, since the innovative firm describes itself as a team of "creative problem-solvers who work with visionary clients in need of better experiences and environments for themselves and the people they serve."[6]

Taking the idea of collaboration literally, the folks from the medical center and Kahler Slater met regularly for visioning sessions, along with members of the Farmington community. Their goal was to create an environmental experience that would not only meet the physical needs of patients, but would be true to the values of the hospital staff. In addition, they wanted to produce a design that honored the spirit of Native American tradition without infringing on the culture and beliefs of the Christian community.

Thanks to open dialogue based on mutual respect, even when different matters of faith and beliefs could have made the cultural divide difficult to cross, many concerns were brought to the forefront. Where there might well have been a battle based on lack of trust and competing agendas, there was genuine respect. When financial stressors might have killed the aesthetic elements so crucial to the end result, the teams worked together and got a sales surcharge passed by a community that recognized the value of the project. Jennifer Schlimgen, architect and "Experience Designer" at Kahler Slater, recalls that there had previously been two referendums for the community to share in the costs of the hospital expansion, and both had failed. "So it was their third try at getting the tax passed. We created a video with a professional videographer to basically make the case for the community as to why the hospital was important. So they went out to Rotary Clubs, Kiwanis, and Chamber of Commerce meetings and sought people out. They did a ton of work to engage the community."[7] On the third try, the referendum won in a landslide!

The result was a new wing with a beautiful spa-like atmosphere, including a piano in the entryway, bright sunlight, open spaces, water features, graceful curved walls, and environmental touches not often found in a hospital. Schlimgen notes that the Kahler Slater team was fortunate to have the early counsel of a half-Navajo, half-Hopi advisor who sagely suggested that the architects not try to over-accommodate the Navajos, saying, "If you make it special for us, someone else will be unhappy. Just make it okay for us to be there."[8]

With that in mind, the architects created the showcase feature of the new wing based on the sacred structure of the *hogan*, which literally means "home place" and in the Navajo tradition is a circular one-room dwelling. The four posts of the hogan are oriented to the north, south, east, and west. The medical center's hogans were built at intervals throughout the addition. Symbolic of the Navajo traditions, to the Western or Christian eye they were simply beautiful structures that allowed people to gather comfortably for purposes of prayer, conversation, or classroom instruction. Says Schlimgen, "We picked the circular form and the four cardinal points in the oculus at the top based on the hogan, but if you didn't know anything about Navajo culture, you would just think it was a pretty round room. So it satisfied the Navajos, but there is nothing particularly Native American or Navajo about it, that's just how it is."[9]

Another issue that was solved by the new structure was one that had long troubled Navajos who worked at the hospital. According to their religious beliefs, they were not supposed to pass by a morgue where dead bodies were housed, yet in the older structure, there was no way to avoid that. Kahler Slater accommodated this religious prohibition by creating an entrance that only those people who were intentionally entering the morgue need access and others could easily bypass.

Even more remarkable, the collaborating teams were able to determine how to deal with the thorny issue of Navajo tribe members being forced to spend their last moments of life alone. In their ingenious plan for the new wing, the Kahler Slater group was able to incorporate a large number of private rooms with screened-in balconies that opened directly to the outside in order to allow the departing spirits to move heavenward. With that change, both family members and hospital staff could be at the bedside in the last moments of a patient's life. Thanks to Kahler Slater's skillful design and the willing collaboration of the SJRMC's engineering staff, the hospital was able to build the overhanging balconies to shade the desert-facing rooms below, keeping the energy costs of cooling and heating the balcony additions manageable.

ENVIRONMENTS THAT ELICIT COLLABORATION

Given the Kahler Slater team's penchant for crafting creative environments, it makes perfect sense that one of their must-haves for their own headquarters in Milwaukee was a slip for their pontoon boat called, aptly enough, *The Experience.* A favorite spot for staff meetings and client conferences, apparently there's nothing quite like a sunset cruise to get the creative juices flowing and keep the customers coming back for more.

After Kahler Slater was recognized eight times in a row as a *Great Place to Work®* in the *Small & Medium Workplaces* category by a collective comprising *Entrepreneur* and *HR* magazines and The Best Place to Work Institute in San Francisco, they decided to study the common factors that made for great environmental experiences. The Kahler Slater team met with the other Best Place to Work award winners to see how each company's physical workplace, in combination with the social and cultural aspects of the organization, played a role in their success. Their theory started with the supposition that great companies inherently understand that the strategic and efficient use of space is a huge contributor to collaboration and overall productivity, and not just an outdated notion about bestowing the corner office as a sign of status. The desire to test this theory prompted the Kahler Slater folks to visit multiple companies, ultimately compiling their findings about the physical characteristics of a well-designed workplace.[10]

It's not just their specific findings that are so fascinating, but how you can begin to see the relevance of physical space and layout as an underpinning of a collaborative culture. As you'll see in a moment, it's far more than mere proximity to each other that gets people interacting in a positive manner. And the fact that a busy company at the top of its game would go to such lengths to share its research with others speaks volumes about how serious Kahler Slater is about collaboration—even with strangers.

At Kahler Slater, everyone works in a cubicle, and the conference rooms, which are plentiful, are used for focused work, phone calls, or large gatherings. There's a wine bar in the corner where the staff holds receptions, gathers for lunch, does a group crossword puzzle, and meets most days at 4 pm for something—or nothing. "Last Friday was Nice Day at 4, because it was a nice day. There is a great deal of collaboration, communication, and fun that happens in that environment," says Schlimgen.[11] Sounds nice, all right.

See which of the following attributes are evident in your workplace and which you might do well to take into further consideration. Even in a home office or small business setting, recognizing what contributes to productivity can influence simple but significant decisions, such as what kind of lamps or window treatments to buy, where to place your computers, or how to arrange your overall physical space.

HOW DOES YOUR SPACE STACK UP?

Despite the emergence of the open-space cubicle world, the objective of these supposedly egalitarian workplaces is probably more a function of keeping costs down than encouraging people to collaborate. In actuality, the need for distraction-free environments is essential to productivity, a requirement that Kahler Slater meets by providing multiple conference rooms for different uses and group sizes. According to the Buffalo Organization for Social and Technological Innovation, most of us are engaged in solo "head down" tasks for approximately half of our workday.[12] Thus, having a workplace that provides some (if not total) privacy, white noise, and available-to-all private spaces such as conference rooms or patios is critical for top performance. Conversely, given the emphasis most companies put on teamwork, having spaces that accommodate group activities like project meetings or brainstorming sessions is also important. But what some companies may overlook is the need for spontaneous interaction in informal lounges or cafes that can offer conversational opportunities that might not happen in a more formal or disconnected setting.

With as much time as most of us spend on the job, it's important to honor our unique personalities and preferences when we can, especially in our immediate space, if not in the common areas. Taking into account right- or left-handedness seems obvious, but ask a leftie who's been forced to work at a right-handed desk for a decade, and you'll see that it's not something that's always done. As someone who spends hours in front of a computer each day, I can tell you firsthand how critical proper ergonomics in your chair and keyboard, as well as task lighting and placement of phone, printer, and electronics, can be for both comfort and efficiency. And why would you want to pay for health-related problems like chronic back pain if you can prevent them in the first place?

Many companies go a step further in terms of personalization, allowing their employees to completely customize their workstation or office, as long as it's not offensive to others. If you take the tour, led by a "culture guide," of Zappos.com's famously quirky headquarters in Nevada, you'll see Tiki hut and Mardi Gras–inspired cubicle decor, including jungle foliage, hanging beads, and dorm room–like rock posters. While not all companies may be in favor of flying their freak flags quite as high as Zappos, the days of restricting personal touches like family photos, plants, or office toys are long gone, as well they should be.

Ideally, balancing structural features such as access to daylight, lack of glare, and temperature control with optimal physical layout can maximize workflow. Consider the proximity of individuals and teams that routinely work together, as well as access to support people and technical capabilities that make work life easier and more pleasant. Factor in the frequent office shifts and physical moves of employees, and you'll see that furniture and technology that adapt easily to change can make life easier while keeping costs down. Finally, in what Kahler Slater rather poetically terms "clear wayfinding," you'll want to ensure that people not only find their destinations easily but also intersect in places that encourage interaction, such as hallways, open paths, and alcove-adjacent spaces.

Of course, this kind of engineered interaction can go a bit too far, such as when Steve Jobs was deep in the design plans for a new Apple office building and insisted that there be only one men's restroom and one women's restroom so people would be forced to, well, bump into each other on their way to the loo. Not surprisingly, his staff rebelled at this suggestion, and Jobs relented, adding a second bath for each gender.

THE CONFIDENT COLLABORATEUR

It takes more than proximity and space planning, no matter how skillfully executed, to foster a culture of collaboration. Having worked with numerous teams from around the globe at companies such as PayPal, Avery Dennison, Warner Bros, Microsoft, and many more, I find that people are often reluctant to collaborate or even engage in open conversation because they fear that they have nothing to contribute or will be judged harshly by their colleagues. Sometimes they're concerned that unless their ideas are nothing short of groundbreaking, they should keep their mouths shut. But if you've hung around C-suites as long as I have, you know that moments of earth-shattering brilliance are few and far between, and that most interaction is simply meant to move the ball a little farther down the field. Which is fine. After all, that's what drives commerce.

Still, it doesn't hurt to prime the pump of collaboration with a few conversational tweaks that can encourage authentic dialogue, build trust, and lay the groundwork for dealing successfully with conflict. Here's a simple but effective technique to get people talking on a deeper level than business-as-usual.

IDENTIFYING YOUR CREDIBILITY BOOSTERS

All of us have something unique about ourselves that in our private mythology makes us feel special. Often we choose to share that talent or accomplishment—and our feelings about it—only with those closest to us. But what happens when we are asked to identify something that makes us unique? First, the pressure is off because it's not us self-promoting—someone else is insisting that we toot our own horn. Second, we have to think about not only what that unique element is but also how best to articulate that special something.

Learning to appropriately highlight your accomplishments is nothing short of an art form, but it's worth working at. After all, haven't we all marveled at those people who seem to have gotten ahead simply because others are aware of their contributions? I'm not suggesting that we shamelessly plug our successes (although there's a time for that, too), but rather that we find graceful ways to ensure that others recognize our value.

Here's one way you can begin to build that muscle for yourself and your team. This technique works well in a group meeting, strategy session, or even a conference, particularly when people don't know each other well or are meeting for the first time. Invite participants to split into pairs or small groups. Have each person share a "Credibility Booster" with his or her partner, that is, a personal or professional accomplishment that he or she finds particularly meaningful. It's likely that this is something known to friends and family but not necessarily to colleagues.

Generally, people will ask a lot of questions about what they should or shouldn't highlight, but it's important that you allow them to be the arbiters of what constitutes a "meaningful accomplishment." Making judgments about our own value is the foundation of personal branding, and it's a critical skill whether you operate in the executive or entrepreneurial ranks. This exercise can help you determine the unique differentiators that make you stand out in a sea of competitors, both internal and external.

Give each person a couple of minutes to highlight his story to his partner and then reverse roles and have the other person share her accomplishment. If this is a new group or team that will be spending some time together, have everyone introduce their partner to the group at large, rather than themselves, by relaying the details of who their partner is and what he or she does, as well as his or her Credibility Booster. While at first some people will be a little shy about sharing, when they hear their story told aloud by someone else, not only will they bond with the group, but the experience will open the door to natural self-disclosure.

Some of the jaw-dropping examples I've heard include a tech executive who won the notoriously difficult cold-water swim across the San Francisco Bay to Alcatraz—not once, but twice. Or the young woman who casually let it slip that she was a former rocket scientist, a fact she'd never considered might be relevant, or even interesting, to others. Then there was the fellow who just happened to have his doctorate in English literature, unbeknownst to his colleagues. Or the woman who'd started a restaurant and a non-profit while still in her twenties as a means of helping feed the homeless in her home country.

I've heard people modestly tell stories about physical obstacles overcome, families cared for, academic achievements, awards, and a multitude of impressive credits—often accomplished while holding down a demanding day job. Interestingly, no matter how impressive the accomplishment, I am routinely asked, "Do people care about that?" or "Do I seem arrogant if I mention this?" Yes, people do care, if only because it makes them more comfortable sharing their own story. And, no, told with humility and truthfulness, people who disclose accomplishments of which they're genuinely proud seem anything but arrogant.

CREATORS PROJECT

Organizations nurture collaborative cultures in a variety of ways, from funneling traffic through common corridors to floating down the Milwaukee River. Sometimes just giving people free time to daydream and create whatever they are passionate about fosters collaboration. Google has famously instituted their "20% Time," which lets technologists use up to 20 percent of their workweek to research unassigned projects that are of interest to them. Those projects, which insiders say are monitored more by culture than by time clocks, have spawned successes including Gmail, AdSense, and Google News. But it was actually global giant 3M that first made the idea stick when a salesman named Richard Drew, experimenting on his own time, invented masking tape.

Sometimes the best collaborations come from unlikely partnerships, such as when Fortune 500 stalwart Intel hooked up with snarky Vice Media to explore an idea at the intersection of art and technology.[13] Vice, once a free monthly newspaper catering to hipsters and music fans in New York's Lower East Side, is now a global content company headquartered in Brooklyn's cool Williamsburg neighborhood. The sprawling online company includes print, music, television, film, and online news divisions operating in more than 30 countries. With an irreverent style aimed at young people, Vice is the industry leader in the creation of original online videos and covers arts, media, politics, news, technology, and more.

According to urban legend surrounding Vice's bad-boy boss Shane Smith, it all started when his buddy, director/producer Spike Jonze, asked Smith what he would do if he had no financial constraints. Smith responded that he would set up a series of modern-day events based on the salons of Paris circa 1920 where artists, musicians, writers, and filmmakers could come together in a mash-up of creative collaboration. At the least, they'd have the opportunity to view one another's work. At best, the interaction would start a rich multicultural creative exchange with hip individuals and organizations.

When Intel recognized the potential of connecting with people who were using computers not just for technological support but to actually drive new ideas and innovations, they signed on to solve the "no financial constraints" piece of the puzzle. The Creators Project kicked off in San Francisco in 2012 as a cultural festival of art installations, concerts, screenings, panel discussions, parties, and more. Sort of a TED meets Coachella meets MacWorld meets E3.

Since its smash debut, the Creators Project has toured the globe, holding events in São Paulo, Paris, Beijing, Seoul, and New York. They've showcased more than 150 artists and entertained thousands of participants with bands like Interpol and Animal Collective. So what do Intel and Vice stand to gain by their unusual pairing? Both believe that by encouraging people to use their computers to create rather than merely consume, they create loyal fans. Vice leads the way in showing artists how they can accomplish their goals by introducing them to cutting-edge creators who are using computers in intriguing new ways. And Intel provides the technology and financial support—all branded in a low-key rather than an in-your-face way that appeals to artists and hipster tech geeks alike.

As the iconoclastic Smith told *Wired* magazine about the partnership, which began with exploratory meetings about how Vice could partner with Intel, "Vice started when, basically, idiots were allowed to publish. Desktop publishing and technology allowed us to start our own magazine, and then when we started VBS [the video division], cheap editing equipment, cheap cameras, and cheap, usable software allowed us to make a network online. Technology has always been at the heart of what we do, and that's why Intel is such a perfect partner. Then, we found all these creators around the world."[14]

CAPTURE THE MINDSHARE SNAPSHOT: CONTINUING THE COLLABORATION

In some companies, when you're out, you're out. Even when you leave on good standing and of your own volition, the party is just plain over. At other organizations, the collaboration continues even after you've moved on. You remain respectful colleagues or even good friends, freely sharing information and connections. But how do you handle it when someone wants to come back to the fold? How do you turn what could be an awkward explanation into a cause for celebration?

CHALLENGE

For companies like Kahler Slater that thrive on transparency and trust, inviting a great employee to come back after she has left to pursue another opportunity is a no-brainer. Why wouldn't you want the good talent to come back around a second time? But how do you handle the reappearance so it makes sense to people who may not have been privy to the particulars of the departure, let alone the reappearance? What is the best means of communication to clear up any misconceptions and stop gossip before it starts?

TACTICS

Hold an awards ceremony, of course! At Kahler Slater, when a valued employee returns to the company, they see it as a cause for celebration. After all, these guys are ready to celebrate a nice day. The entire company gets together, and the returnee is presented with "The Sacred Boomerang." The returning employee tells everyone what she has been up to since leaving and what she will be doing next. This not only acknowledges that it's okay to make changes in your career but that if you're good at what you do and there's a job available for you, you'll be welcomed back into the fold.[15]

MORE

Learn about more celebrations, awards, and events that smart companies use to kick off collaboration at www.LibbyGill.com, and see what you can incorporate to make your work a little more fun.

Next, let's look at ways that you can *Connect* your product, service, cause, or idea to the widest possible relevant arena. Richer and more nuanced than basic networking, these ideas will demonstrate how you can elevate your brand conversations to a higher level than you ever have before.

Chapter Four

CONNECT

Creating the Authentic Emotional Link

Only connect!
—*E. M. Forster,* Howard's End

FIFTY YEARS AFTER HER DEATH, THE LEGEND OF MARILYN MONROE not only lives on but has blossomed into a full-fledged brand. In addition to the obvious Hollywood paraphernalia such as movie posters, Marilyn's image adorns cosmetics, fragrances, key chains, mouse pads, puzzles, dolls, wall clocks, blankets, and beach towels, to name just a few. There's also a Marilyn-inspired television series with talk of a live musical version to follow. Now, with a line of Marilyn-themed cafes and luxury spas in the works, the brand appears to be unstoppable.

Leveraging the image of glamour and enduring style, Orlando-based Marilyn Monroe Spas plans to open several business lines in cooperation with the company that owns the bulk of the Monroe estate. These will include a nail boutique, offering the usual assortment of manicure, pedicure, and waxing services; a chain of "glamour rooms," providing hair and makeup styling along with photography sessions; and luxury spas in locations such as resort hotels and cruise ships. Company co-founder Niki Bryan described the spa brand to the *Los Angeles Times* as "the kind of high-glamour, high-elegance, high-touch environment that we believe will represent the relaxed, pampering side of her personality." Adds partner and co-founder Al Weiss, former president of worldwide operations at Walt Disney Parks and Resorts, "We want this to be a fairly elegant, high-quality product with a distinctive design that has an old Hollywood feel. When people walk in they're going to see her red lips, they're going to see things that they'll recognize very quickly from an iconic standpoint, and they'll know they've walked into a world of Marilyn."[1]

My question is: Why do we care about walking into the world of Marilyn Monroe and not, for instance, the world of Jayne Mansfield or Rita Hayworth? Certainly these women were accomplished actresses and famous sex symbols, just as Marilyn was. They lived in the era of Old Hollywood glamour, just as she did. And yet they haven't been immortalized nearly to the degree that Marilyn has. What was it about Marilyn Monroe that continues to make people want to connect to her, albeit in a completely commercialized way?

PROCESSING EMOTIONS

In order to understand the basis for connection, we need to take a quick peek inside the brain to see how we process emotions. The brain is by far the most complicated organ in our body, and although our knowledge about its functioning is increasing at a rapid pace—thanks in great part to improvements in fMRI scanners and other medical equipment—it is still not completely understood by scientists. What we do know is that different areas of the brain process and control our emotions, affecting the way we feel and the way we behave. When these areas are functioning and interacting properly, we are thought to be emotionally healthy. When any areas of the brain malfunction, serious problems can result. In fact, much of the brain research to date has been conducted on patients with brain injuries because these allow scientists to ascertain what happens when one part of the brain is damaged and unable to function on its own or in proper coordination with other parts of the brain.

DEEP LIMBIC SYSTEM

Referred to as the DLS, the deep limbic system is like the central warehouse and processing unit for our emotional memories, both positive and negative. Emotionally charged memories can sometimes be stockpiled for life and can have a deep and lasting impact on our overall outlook and personality. Negative memories—fear in particular—are often so powerful that scientists call the phenomenon of their long-term storage "fear memory consolidation." In that process, we actually build memory upon memory so that together the memories sometimes greatly outweigh the precipitating incident.

PREFRONTAL CORTEX

The prefrontal cortex (PFC) is the front half of our brains and the seat of focus, impulse control, emotional control, judgment, and empathy. Normal functioning in the PFC helps us to be goal-oriented, conscientious, and considerate of others. But when PFC activity is low, we may feel distracted, unproductive, or even antisocial. In contrast, when the PFC is overstimulated, it can lead to anxiety or lack of flexibility in our thoughts or behaviors.

AMYGDALA

The amygdala is an almond-shaped area in the temporal lobe, which is the center of strong emotions, including fear and love. This primitive part of the brain, which controls what we've come to know as the fight-or-flight syndrome, helps us make emotional judgments such as whether someone is a friend or foe and thus is critical to our survival.

WHEN WE CONNECT WITH SOMEONE OR SOMETHING so strongly that we "feel it in our gut" or "know it in our heart," it is actually the delicate interplay of these brain functions that is steering our emotions and, consequently, our decision making. Just try telling a BMW lover who is convinced that she must have the "ultimate driving machine" that she would be just as well served with a top-of-the-line Toyota. She is likely to quote all the statistics and consumer reports that back up her decision, which is precisely what the BMW brand (like most brands) has trained us to do. But even though the high-performance fan may actually have accurate and relevant data, she is still making an emotional decision rather than a rational one. She wants to be part of the high-performance luxury car club more than she wants to be part of the sensible, affordable, and totally dependable car club. Her emotions, and therefore beliefs, are in alignment with the BMW brand. Conversely, the sensible car guy who firmly believes that luxury autos are a ridiculous waste of money can probably rattle off the high costs associated with their maintenance and repair, comparing them with the far less expensive repair costs of the car he favors. His values and preferences may likely be more in line with those of Toyota or Honda. Neither opinion is right or wrong. No doubt, mountains of data support either position. The point is: that position starts with emotions that are based on values and backed up by reason.

Marilyn's long-lasting appeal is no different. Those of us who feel an indefinable connection to the star of hits like *Some Like It Hot* and *Gentlemen Prefer Blondes* are responding emotionally to some element of her sensual beauty, raw vulnerability, or scrappy charm. Even without factoring in the dramatic demise that put her on a par with legends like James Dean or Tupac Shakur, that's plenty of grist for the emotional mill. We are pulled. Or we're not. Part of the art of branding is understanding that you can't possibly appeal to everyone, nor should you attempt to. You'll be beating your head against an unmovable brick wall. The key is to unlock the potential for an emotional connection with people whose values align with yours.

Mysterious and elusive, emotions are hard to pin down. Attempt to describe the depth of feeling you have for your child, spouse, or pet and you'll see what I mean. It's difficult to put into words with any accuracy. Now imagine that difficulty multiplied tenfold for a business that not only needs to make that initial emotional connection but then must layer in products, services, delivery methods, return policies, and more. The problem for many brands, however, is that they get right down to business and ignore the nuances of emotion. And without that critical seed of emotional connection, there's little opportunity for a relationship to take root.

CONNECTING WITH OUR WHY

In his insightful book *Start With Why: How Great Leaders Inspire Everyone to Take Action*, author Simon Sinek explores the idea that successful leaders inspire from the inside out rather than the outside in.[2] Sinek contends that the best leaders inspire companies, and consequently customers, by consistently starting with a deep sense of internal purpose: a *why*. Everything that company then does, from the products they sell to the people they hire, springs from their *why*. When customers trust the why of an organization, because of either an instinctive gut feeling or an actual understanding of how the business operates (or both), they are willing to follow the company through thick and thin.

Perhaps no one understands this loyalty better than Dr. Tamara Monosoff, founder of the Mom Invented® brand.[3] Proving the maxim that necessity is the mother of invention—especially when active toddlers are involved—Tamara has created a thriving community for female entrepreneurs and inventors. Like many an invention, however, the creation of this group came about through a rather circuitous route. After working in the White House for three years and then moving with her husband to Hong Kong, where she finished her doctorate in women and leadership, Tamara became pregnant with her first child. Wanting to be closer to family, the Monosoffs returned stateside, where their daughter Sophia was born.

Ten months later, Sophia had discovered the joy of pulling toilet paper off the roll and stuffing it down the toilet. Tamara, meantime, was pulling out her hair and searching the stores for a baby lock to secure the toilet paper roll—but none existed. Not one to be defeated by a mere detail, Tamara created, manufactured, and marketed the TP Saver®, saving not only the toilet paper but also the sanity of countless parents.

Tamara's *why* started with the simple desire to solve what she figured was a problem that many mothers faced. What she discovered was an entire community of creative moms eager to share the journey of working motherhood and, more specifically, the invention of consumer products that made their job as parents a little easier. Things kicked into high gear when Tamara sent out a free press release on PRWeb.com that resulted in an invitation for her to appear on the *Today* show with Katie Couric. Tamara recalls, "What was so interesting for me was that, after being on the show for less than two minutes, I had over half a million people, mostly moms, come to my website. But they weren't interested in my product. They were interested in how I did it." Tamara decided to share her journey, mistakes and all, by writing the *Mom Inventors Handbook*, which was followed by four more books, including her latest, *How Hot Is Your Product: 10 Easy Steps to Determine If Your Product Will Be a Hit.*

Tamara reflects back on her initial inspiration to become an inventor:

> I had these two little kids, and I remember sitting on my couch and thinking, here I had worked in the White House—and all of a sudden I'm home. Ten years ago, when you typed in "mom inventor" or "mom entrepreneur," nothing came up in Google. There wasn't that type of

support. I said to myself, "Okay, I'm an intelligent person, there are a lot of moms out there who are intelligent and creative, and I want to celebrate that." I wanted this brand to have that kind of meaning— the logo is in a circle to show community and support for each other through this process.

On every package, there's a picture of me inviting women to participate in our Mom Invented community. So if you picked up our Good Bites Crustless Sandwich Cutter in the bread aisle of the grocery store, you'd flip it over, see the mom, and realize that there is a community. All the products are about solving common everyday problems, but it's really not just about the product. It's about the whole backstory.

That backstory not only connects, but endears, Tamara to a huge community of women with whom she freely—and I mean that literally as well as metaphorically—shares vast stores of information and resources to help them see their ideas to fruition. But it's not just goodwill and girl power that helps these women connect to each other and to their customers. There's a ton of heavy lifting involved in building vibrant relationships.

Tamara compounds her personal expertise by featuring other successful entrepreneurs on her blog and website. While she's happy to hear about their successes, she's even more interested in sharing how they've overcome challenges because those are the stories from which her audience learns the most. Having a structure that allows her to share an ongoing stream of information is critical—and duplicable by any business of any size. She uses her blog as the basis for connection and then layers in Twitter and Facebook. Tamara is particularly fond of Twitter because it's easy to use, and she believes people respond better to bite-size nuggets of information. She has also learned firsthand that members of the media who frequent Twitter are always looking for a great story. Her moms of invention have learned how to fill that need by offering a compelling hook in 140 characters.

As evidenced by Tamara's success, the key to creating deep and lasting connections is to balance inspiration and information. "Don't, however," she cautions her community, "fall too much in love with your idea. People think this is my *one* idea. But when you're so focused on one product, all of your energy, time, everything is going into that and you're not open to other possibilities. I always say, no, this is not a child. This is a product. You'll be amazed at what happens when you let go. A space opens for new ideas, and your creativity percolates again."

MINDSHARE MINUTE: CRAFTING YOUR WHY MESSAGE

Drill down to discover the *why* of your business. Answer these questions to help you clarify your *why*, first for yourself and then so you'll be able to communicate it to clients and customers. You can also visit the Mindshare section at www.LibbyGill.com for a detailed description on how to craft your *Why* Message.

1. Why are you compelled to do the work you do?
2. What feeling do you evoke in your customers?
3. How does your business change people's lives?
4. What would others miss out on if you were not in business?

BORN TO WORK HERE

Headquartered in Sidney, Nebraska, Cabela's® is the World's Foremost Outfitter® of fishing, hunting, and outdoor gear. With a thriving direct marketing operation and 40 retail stores that do double-duty as wildlife education centers, Cabela's employs more than 12,000 people in the United States and Canada—although to label them *employees* may be a bit of an understatement. A *why* company in which the people truly believe in the product and want to share their passion, Cabela's employees are more akin to ambassadors of the great outdoors than they are sales professionals.

Despite their dedication, when Cabela's hired Thomas Millner as its new CEO in 2009 during one of the worst economic climates in recent history, he wanted to revitalize the team in order to maintain sales momentum in the highly competitive retail environment. To help him map out a strategy, Millner brought in Kenexa, the human capital experts we met in Chapter Two. Millner and Kenexa knew they had a strong employee base on which to build. Now they needed to discover what drew employees to work at Cabela's in the first place, what tools employees needed to excel, and how the company's leadership could help create lifelong career opportunities for its workforce.

Kenexa's mission was to help Cabela's shift their culture to a work-smarter mindset so they could maintain momentum and build the bottom line. The company didn't plan to do this through discounts, rebates, or any other traditional marketing means. While those incentives work in the short term, they seldom create long-term loyalty—and the same maxim holds true for employees. Instead, Kenexa decided to help Cabela's make a deeper connection with the strongest asset in its arsenal—the passion of its own workforce.[4]

Although perhaps not as sexy as Prada or Moet & Chandon, Cabela's nonetheless has a *why* that is every bit as strong as the *why* of those luxury brands: specifically, to share a passion for the outdoors with others. When Kenexa's employment branding team embarked on an investigation to identify the essence of Cabela's culture, they discovered that most of the employees felt such a deep connection to the company that they considered their work more of a calling than a job or even a career. One employee actually said he was "born to work at Cabela's." The challenge, then, was to channel all that passion in a more productive direction so Cabela's could increase the bottom line, even during a recession.

Using many of the same principles that companies use to connect with external customers, Kenexa's team created an employee branding program designed to recruit, hire, and retain top performers who shared that passion for the outdoors but also had the skills to succeed in retail. Those two critical factors—not always found side by side—made all the difference. Kenexa helped Cabela's create an employee value proposition (EVP) that they titled "The Nature of Cabela's," which is summed up in the five core tenets you see below. As Cabela's states on its company website, "The Nature of Cabela's is meant to describe what it's like to work here. It is the product of hours of employee interviews at all levels—it is an authentic description of Cabela's culture, but also an aspirational depiction of where we are headed as we continue to grow."[5]

Rather than creating these core concepts, Cabela's and the Kenexa team listened to what employees were already saying about the company's authentic values. They then mined that dialogue to compose the five cornerstones of the Cabela's brand:

THE NATURE OF CABELA'S

- We are proud of the brand we've built.
- Our passion is for the outdoors and the people who play there.
- Our standards are very high.
- We work very hard.
- We were born to work here.

In language that cleverly captured the brand essence, Kenexa created a "Field Guide" that managers used to roll out the value statements to employees companywide, soliciting success stories and sharing them on their website. At the same time, Kenexa designed an employee recruitment campaign, even creating a "Culture Quiz" on their website that asked, "Were You Born to Work Here?"—a question that lets candidates self-select if they want to proceed with the process.

Within a year, Cabela's employee engagement scores had increased 5 percent. Engagement scores of employees who viewed the Nature of Cabela's campaign favorably were more than double the scores of those who had a negative or neutral reaction to the process. Furthermore, managers whose groups had high engagement scores were tapped to mentor those managers whose groups had low scores. The low-scoring groups' engagement numbers rose 21 percent the following year. But the most important metric for the retail company was the sales per labor hour score, which is a productivity measure that quantifies the total dollars of sales for every labor hour worked.

As the engagement scores rose throughout the company, so did the sales per labor hour. In fact, among stores that ranked in the top fiftieth percentile of engagement scores, sales per labor hour rose 9.3 percent over the sales of those stores in the lower half of the engagement rankings. While percentage numbers in the single digits may not sound impressive to those untrained in retail, this figure translates into millions of dollars per year in increased sales. As Millner succinctly summed it up, "If we don't pay attention to our engagement scores, we're doing so at our own peril."[6]

RIGHT FROM THE START

Ask any salesperson who knows his stuff, and he will tell you that it can take a dozen or more *touches*—or interactions—including emails, phone calls, newsletters, or in-person meetings, before you begin to build a relationship with a prospect. Typically, the more complex or expensive your product, the longer the sales cycle and the more touches are required to build awareness, rapport, connection, and trust.

Your organizational brand is no different, except that instead of selling a specific product or service, you are creating a connection between your prospect and your company. If you think of this relationship-building process as a series of connective touch points with your customer, you can begin to see all the opportunities that you have to make an impression. My favorite salespeople are those who see the process not as a painful series of start-stop conversations but as a series of connections that lead to partnership. And my favorite companies are those that start the relationship off on the right foot—with open communication and top-notch service—and then continue to build from there.

Far too many companies spend their time and energy prospecting and closing new clients and then hand them off to a lower-level associate, with the person who sealed the deal never to be heard from again. Not that junior team members shouldn't be involved—they should—but don't send your client the message that now that you've gotten them signed and their check has cleared, your heavy lifting is over. They need to know that you're with them every step of the way, even if, in fact, the junior folks are doing most of the day-to-day work. And if you've got account executives or staffers who will be integral to the customer relationship on a regular basis, make sure your client is comfortable with them from the initial meeting.

Here are some ideas for establishing your brand right from the start, providing your customers with personality and panache, as they deserve:

- **Blow their minds with a branded welcome packet.** Just letting your customers know that you actually have a process to get them set up, serviced, and clear about next steps sends a message about how serious you are about taking care of business—their business, that is. Provide documents, contact lists, and technical data in a cohesive, professionally designed print and/or digital package.

- **Introduce the team**. Set an introductory in-person phone or Skype meeting and get your new client acquainted with anyone who will be touching their business. Give an overview of your roles, background, and how each team member will contribute to their success. This can also be a great time to set expectations and establish a communications flow, including scheduling meetings, dealing with paperwork, and handling everything from day-to-day basics to client emergencies.

- **Clarify the outcome**. Soon after, if not at, the first meeting, you'll want to plant the end goal of the project firmly in the mind of your client. If you don't define success, your client can't possibly recognize it when you achieve it. Agree on a clear outcome, including a range from acceptable to ideal results, especially if these results include things not in your control. For example, a responsible publicist may tell you how she plans to position your business with the media, the action steps she will take, and the relationships she has in place, but she will be unlikely to promise you the front page of *Time* magazine or a *New York Times* bestseller. When you clearly qualify and quantify the anticipated outcome, you do everything in your power to deliver—that's when you get continued business and referrals.

- **Assign homework**. My clients love it when they know not only what is expected of me but also exactly what is expected of them.

If appropriate, assign homework, reading, workshops—anything that is relevant to your customer's business growth. The only caveat is that most professionals are incredibly busy people, so your assignments must be worth the effort and/or must provide a pathway to freeing up more of their valuable time.

- **Surprise and delight.** While your customers may expect a little something for a birthday or special occasion, a surprise gift at the beginning of your relationship can really set you apart (and pave the way for referrals). It shouldn't be so elaborate that it embarrasses them, but it should be significant—and relevant— enough to be meaningful. When a new speaker bureau brings me on board, we'll send a beautiful handmade candle wrapped in silk from the Yvonne White Collection. Or we'll order a super-trendy fashion or homeware item from colleague Carolyn Akel's Coco's Closet. And when a client mentions a favorite author, musician, or winery, that information goes right into the future surprise file for another celebratory occasion.

MINDSHARE MINUTE: BUILDING A BRANDED INTRODUCTION PACKAGE

Build a branded introduction package, including contact sheets, homework assignments, technical instructions, legal documents, and anything else your client needs to get started. It's well worth the small investment to hire a designer to create a cohesive look that includes your logo, a proper font, and all the graphic elements that show you pay attention to details. If your marketing budget is minimal (or even if it's not), check out 99Designs.com or Elance. com for some great designers at a discount.

CONNECTING WITH YOUR
INNER ENTREPRENEUR

The most successful professionals are connected professionals. It just stands to reason that the people who:

- know what's happening in their industry as well their company,
- know who the hot players are (and aren't),
- have built a reputation for being a great resource for colleagues, and
- who can borrow best practices from friendly competitors

are going to be the go-to people for your business. Consider the contrary, for example, like the chief financial officer (CFO) who's great with numbers but not so great with people. Odds are that the CFO, no matter how good a data-cruncher he may be, has a ceiling on how valuable he is in the long run. It's hard to help build a brand when you rarely come out of your cubicle or corner office.

I frequently coach professionals who are so busy dealing with day-to-day challenges that they convince themselves that spending time creating connections is a luxury instead of a necessity. In order to create the kinds of relationships that can result in long-term value for you and others, however, you have to put in some time and effort. But it's critical to have those relationships in place before you need them, not when you're desperate for help. Fortunately, technology can keep those ties alive and thriving without a lot of wasted motion.

A master at making meaningful connections, Reid Hoffman is the co-founder of LinkedIn, the largest professional networking service in the world. With the early career intention of becoming an academic, lucky for us, Hoffman saw the promise of a bigger platform as an entrepreneur and focused his efforts on building businesses with the possibility of massive scale. (Note his *why* right there.) The list of companies in which he has played a key strategic role reads like a who's who of Silicon Valley: PayPal, Facebook, Flickr, Pandora, Dropbox, Zynga, and Mozilla, among others.

In his bestselling book *The Start-up of You,* co-written with author and entrepreneur Ben Casnocha, Hoffman contends that in order to succeed, you must manage your career as though you are an entrepreneur in perpetual start-up mode. That means staying nimble, investing in your own learning and growth, taking intelligent risks, and building your professional network. By staying in a state of what Hoffman calls "permanent beta," we are constantly evolving and reinventing not only our careers but also ourselves. And our growth is good news for our organization. The more we know—in terms of people and information—the more we can contribute.[7]

Best of all, we don't have to do it all alone, nor should we. By consciously creating relationships with a diverse mix of people, we build a network that we can tap into for ideas, resources, and further connections. The following are some ideas based on Hoffman and Casnocha's networking concepts that you can easily incorporate into your own business development strategy.

- **Start an association.** You may have thought about it, but when was the last time you actually made the effort to bring together a high-level group of likeminded people with common interests and challenges? By transcending the networking-as-usual trap and getting at some deeper issues, you keep relationships alive and bring new people to the table.
- **Invest in an "intriguing people" fund.** Put some money aside so you can get acquainted with people you want to get to know. Invite them out for coffee or a glass of wine,

take them to lunch, or jump on a plane and meet with them in person. Nothing lets a person know you're serious about building a relationship like flying cross-country to take them out to dinner.

- **Become the connector you want to see in the world.** Most of us have the good fortune to know people who somehow manage to introduce us to the right person at the right time. It's not an accident; it's a skill. By becoming one of those great connectors yourself, the benefits will circle back to you when you help others who are looking for investor money, ideas for projects, or simply a warm introduction to someone they'd like to meet. When you become a hub to other people's relationships, you not only help them (whether you get immediate payback is beside the point), but you put yourself in the flow of information and opportunity.

THE MAGIC OF MIRAVAL

Travel & Leisure magazine calls Miraval "one of the world's top destination resorts." Located on 400 acres near Tucson's Santa Catalina Mountains, Miraval promotes a life in balance through its beautiful accommodations, spa treatments, wellness programs, and healthy cuisine. Individual guests and business groups from all over the world visit the spa for the natural splendor of the Sonoran Desert setting, as well as the roster of award-winning spa activities.

While the guest experience is consistently memorable, it is the unique culture that is truly the basis of Miraval's brand. According to Miraval CEO Michael Tompkins:

Miraval culture can be defined as community-centric and very nurturing. At Miraval, employees serve as teachers, guides, or facilitators of information and experiences that can often be life-altering. Miraval is built on the philosophies of mindfulness and living in the moment. We are known for authenticity and encouraging our employees to be who they are, which in turn creates a unique service dynamic that is relational, rather than one of servitude as you'd find in most hotels or resorts. In this way, our staff serves as co-creators of the guest experience, versus deliverers or presenters of the guest experience. Our service style is unscripted, and employees are given a great deal of latitude to be their unique, true selves.[8]

It is precisely that style of allowing employees to co-create the guest experience rather than serve it up that taps into the entrepreneurial dynamic. By not only allowing but encouraging staff to bring their ideas forward and giving them the opportunity to turn those ideas into new programs and services for guests, the team at Miraval is continually challenged to evolve and expand their professional repertoire. It's a three-way win, with clients benefiting because the programs are always improving, staff benefiting because they get to express their authentic creativity and passion, and Miraval benefiting because this employee approach helps the company recruit and retain the best talent.

At Miraval, three key ingredients of emotional engagement make up the foundation of the brand: anticipation, trust, and joy. (It's worth noting that the San Juan Regional Medical Center also cites anticipation as a core factor in their patient experience.) Miraval defines anticipation as a sense of excitement and optimism—a core belief that great things are on the horizon for the company and its employees. Trust is their fundamental key to connection, with transparency as its basis. Finally, they define joy as a focus on having a healthy and mindful lifestyle, which includes plenty of fun and laughter at work every single day.

Similar to Cabela's culture, the team at Miraval truly gets to live out their passions. As Tompkins says, "Our hiking guides, for instance, would be out on the trails each day whether we were paying them or not. Same with our yogis, our equine staff, our photographers, and so on. Employees tell us over and over that they really appreciate being able to make a positive difference for others, do what they love to do, and build a rewarding career at the same time. Miraval is a place where people go to discover things about themselves unexpectedly, and this happens for our employees as well." And Miraval doesn't just pay lip service to helping their employees explore their passions. Employees are invited to participate in any of the classes, programs, lectures, or activities the company offers. Miraval's leaders believe that by being able to experience the company offerings firsthand, not only do the employees evolve personally, but they are further connected to the core business of the company. As you can imagine, this deep connection to the company ultimately becomes part of the guest experience. After all, there's nothing like authentic loyalty that inspires people to go the extra mile.

BRAND BUILDING BLOCK #3: CREATING THE ONLINE CONNECTION

Other than you yourself, your website is one of the best brand platforms you have for connecting to others. Your site allows you to articulate your core purpose, confirm your credibility, and invite people to interact with you. It can be an efficient way to provide immediate value to prospects and customers through resources like videos, tip sheets, blogs, and more.

Your website is also an effective tool for disqualifying customers who aren't right for your business, which is an extremely useful time-saver, since it spares you and your team from engaging in dialogue, sending proposals, or offering sample products or services to people who aren't potential customers. But it requires that you send a clear message about what you do and for whom you do it. Otherwise, how will people determine whether you're a fit for them? The challenge, of course, is that you've only got about five seconds to help them determine whether it's worth engaging with you further. That's about the average length of time website visitors will stay on your home page before they decide to go elsewhere, a pattern referred to as "bouncing," or decide that they wish to read on and learn more about you.

In my decade of web branding, I've seen just about every mistake one can make online. Fortunately, most of these errors are pretty easy to fix or avoid altogether. With just a bit of diligence and follow-through, you can have a good-looking, functional site that supports your business. The following are the World's Worst Website Woes, as well as some easy ways you can cure these basic branding pitfalls.

LACK OF CLARITY ON YOUR HOME PAGE

Your home page is the most important online real estate you own. It's critical that you use it well. Throughout this chapter, we've been talking about ways you can reinforce the brand vision—that is, the *why*—behind your business in order to connect with your core audience. Your home page is your opportunity to distill your purpose down to a compelling paragraph or two that makes your brand sing. It should be so laser-focused on your *why*, *what*, and *how* that site visitors can't wait to learn more about you and what you can do for them.

CONFUSING SITE NAVIGATION

Confusing site navigation, that is, how you guide visitors to move around within your website, is a common mistake. It usually occurs because, as someone familiar with your business, the way you get from Point A to Point B within your site seems crystal clear to you. But that doesn't mean it's easy or intuitive for others to figure out. If your customers can't easily locate contact numbers, service information, order forms, and other items for which they might be searching, they may simply give up and go away. And you lose a sales opportunity, possibly forever.

Make sure the navigation bar at the top of your site clearly indicates how you find what's inside. If you have cute and catchy navigation button names, make sure they also make the content clear. Check to see that you don't have any broken links within the site, and, above all, put your most important information at the top in a place obvious enough that even the most attention-challenged among us can't miss it.

AMATEURISH DESIGN

Just because your eight-year-old nephew *can* design your site doesn't mean he *should* design your site. Your website needs a professional and polished graphic appeal that's appropriate to your business. Whether you want to evoke a feeling of security and expertise for your insurance brokerage or a funky flair that showcases your vintage clothing store, make sure your website uses current best design practices, including being Americans with Disabilities Act (ADA) compliant. Consider the message you're sending with your color palette, logo, fonts, and other visuals like photos and videos. Don't rely solely on your own design eye, even if it's good—get a consensus from several trusted sources who can give you objective feedback.

Your site doesn't have to win any design awards, but it must have strong visual appeal and be consistent with current practices if you're going to grab and hold people's attention. Some common graphic mistakes to watch out for:

- Tiny little text (that is, less than ten-point font) that makes most people over age 40 run screaming for their reading glasses.
- Lack of contrast, like placing blue text on a green background. If in doubt, black or dark gray text on a light-colored background is by far the most readable color combination. I have a bias against white text on a black background, as it can be difficult to read. If you are using such contrast for drama, just make sure it's legible.
- Watch out for flash that won't read on some computers or complicated images that take too long to load. Your site visitors are impatient. If they have to wait for your graphics, you definitely increase the odds that they might go somewhere else where they don't have to wait around.
- Your photos and other images need to be professional, creative, and relevant. "Clip art" (meaning photos or drawings you buy from photo houses like iStockPhoto.com or

GettyImages.com) are fine, but watch out for visual clichés that you've seen repeatedly, like happy workers high-fiving each other or those little robot people who always seem to be putting the last puzzle piece in place. And make sure that you license photographs legally, as "royalty-free" does not mean free. Be sure you read the fine print.

- Even better, use your own photos—they're original and you don't need legal clearance—but only if they are composed and lit well. Avoid any unprofessional headshots or family photos, even if your site has a homey feel.

LOUSY CONTENT

Now that you've got a good-looking and navigable website, it's time to focus on your content. Too many people spend time, money, and energy making their site look great but forget that the language is equally, if not more, important. After all, which would you rather have: a simple design with rich, engaging content or a site with beautiful design and nothing to say?

In order to establish that all-important emotional connection, you need relevant, original, and well-written content. The descriptive material about you and your business is critical, but it's also important to offer real value to your visitors in the form of articles, videos, white papers, tips, blogs, and resources. After all, you want to be the go-to authority to which your customers will keep coming back over and over again. If you don't have the time or talent to create great content, outsource. One new piece of business, and you've made your investment back.

NOT ESTABLISHING YOUR CREDIBILITY UPFRONT

Failing to establish your credibility can be a total non-starter for securing new business. Your prospect may have found you, but it's still your responsibility to demonstrate your worth. In other words, why do they need what you do? Why is it important for them to have it right now? And why should they buy from you rather than all the other competitors that are just a click away? Build your credibility story with case studies, testimonials, videos, and whatever else is appropriate to the tone and style of your industry. Share value statements that sum up the results that prospects can expect from working with you, using statements such as "I can streamline your online marketing operations in three weeks" or "I guarantee a clutter-free office that will last you six months or I'll come back and reorganize it for free." Then back up your claims with testimonials from satisfied clients—your brand evangelists and de facto sales force. If they love the results you've gotten them, most people are all too happy to share that information with others. If you are in a business like finance or counseling that requires confidentiality, just use initials, general job title, and geographic location. When you have multiple endorsements that have the ring of truth—because they *are* true—people will pay attention.

TOO FEW WAYS TO CONNECT

Once you've gone to all the trouble and expense to build a good-looking, well-written website that gives your customers the information they want, why would you limit the number of ways they can connect to you? Having multiple means of connection allows your community members to choose how they want to interact with you and connect you with others. I'm not suggesting that you spend hours a day as a slave to social media (unless that works for your business), but you should pick two or three platforms that are a good fit for you in terms of reinforcing your brand, keeping current customers up to date, and reaching out to new prospects. Just a few minutes a day on Facebook, Twitter, Pinterest, LinkedIn, Instagram, or whatever works for you can allow you to build two valuable assets: connection and loyalty. If you don't know what online platforms are best for your business, start experimenting. Better yet, hire a college intern for a few hours a week and let him or her experiment under your supervision.

CAPTURE THE MINDSHARE SNAPSHOT: BECOME A MORE CHARISMATIC CONNECTOR

We've all encountered those people who seem to be natural connectors. Not only do they have a kind of effortless magnetism that draws people to them, but they also seem to have an endless supply of contacts whom they're only too eager to share with others. People often cite celebrities like Oprah Winfrey or Bill Clinton as individuals who seem capable of making one-to-one connections everywhere they go—even if they're addressing a huge crowd. Creating relationships is a skill, however, and not an inborn gift. So what lessons can we learn from these charismatic connectors?

CHALLENGE

Margie Aliprandi is one of those natural connectors, although she says she had no idea how to benefit from this ability when she was young. As the single mother of three kids under the age of five and with no sales experience or start-up capital, Margie was desperate for meaningful and well-paid work. And she wanted to do work about which she could feel passionate, which in her case had always been concerned with the idea of helping people grow. For some, it may have been a formidable challenge to help oneself grow in order to help others. For Margie, it was only a matter of time.[9]

TACTICS

Margie decided to try her hand at network marketing, also known as direct sales or multi-level marketing. The company with which she aligned herself makes health, home, and beauty products that are good for people and the planet. In the network marketing business, salespeople are paid commissions not only for products they consume and sell directly to others but also for the sales volume of people they bring into the business. So building a robust team, referred to as a "downline," and helping team members grow as independent entrepreneurs are critical to your own long-term success.

Although the industry has its detractors, Margie is a shining example of how ethical people who provide real value to their customers and teams can build thriving businesses that result in financial freedom. But that level of success requires the ability to connect and communicate with thousands—or, in Margie's case, hundreds of thousands—of people around the world.

Margie's team of nearly 250,000 people comes from 29 different countries, including the United States, Japan, and Malaysia, and has a strong concentration of people in Eurasian areas such as Siberia, Kazakhstan, Uzbekistan, and the Ukraine. Although Margie takes advantage of all the online tools—including websites, social media, email, webcasts, and Skype calls—to stay in touch with her team, she says the most effective way to stay connected is face to face. "Technology has made our world a very small place, yet it's that face-to-face contact that really changes lives," she says. "I know there's value when I can help people learn new skills and strategies, but what really matters is when I meet team members personally and listen to their goals and celebrate their progress, and I can look them in the eye and let them know they're seen and heard. That's where the magic really happens."

Margie recalls the story of a Russian woman named Irina who once came home from the market in tears because she could only afford one apple instead of two. That week, a friend gave Irina a magazine with Margie's story in it. Irina joined Margie's team and eventually met her at a worldwide convention. Irina couldn't speak English and Margie couldn't speak Russian, yet their connection helped create an entirely new life for Irina. "Since then," Margie says, "we've been guests in each other's homes, and Irina has even learned to speak English so we can communicate without a translator."

The last time Irina visited Margie in Utah, Irina had traveled via Japan, where she set up a new team, and then capped off her visit to the United States by speaking almost-fluent English to Margie's team. "It's just so gratifying to see someone step into their inherent greatness," Margie says. "To watch that beautiful growth process unfold—could anything be better? That's as good as it gets."

MORE

Although some charismatic people like Margie are born with energy that can light up a room, you can learn some techniques to make you a better connector. Visit the Mindshare section at www.LibbyGill.com for tips to become a more charismatic connector.

Next, let's look at some *Communication* techniques that can take that initial connection you make with colleagues, clients, and customers to a deeper and broader level. Learn from the professionals how you can establish an ongoing communications strategy to build trust and grow your influence with key constituents.

Chapter Five

COMPETE

What Makes You So Special?

If you don't have a competitive advantage, don't compete.

—Jack Welch

WHAT DOES THE LATIN DANCE–INSPIRED EXERCISE CRAZE CALLED *Zumba*—with millions of global participants joyfully sweating to a mix of hip-hop, salsa, and African rhythms—have in common with Harley-Davidson?

- a. Devotees often wear distinctive garb that identifies them as part of the club.
- b. It represents a free-spirited lifestyle for its passionate fans.
- c. Its brand translates into multiple mediums and consumer experiences.
- d. All of the above.

If you answered *D: All of the above*, you're absolutely right. The story of Zumba all started when fitness guru Alberto "Beto" Perez—then an aspiring dancer—forgot to bring his music to an aerobics class he was teaching in his native Colombia. Instead, he grabbed the one cassette he had with him, which contained Latin music he'd taped off the radio, and improvised his way through the class, combining dance steps with aerobic moves. He soon realized that his students were having fun rather than exercising, and the rest is Zumba Fitness history.[1]

When I first started taking Zumba at my neighborhood YMCA, usually fewer than half a dozen women were in the class. Now, five years later, if you don't get there early, you have to fight for a spot on the dance floor. Unlike the early days, plenty of men are working out alongside the ladies. What made this trend stick when so many other fitness fads fade out before you can say spandex booty shorts?

Zumba Chief Marketing Officer Jeffrey Perlman, brother of CEO and co-founder Alberto Perlman, attributes the company's success to its focus on building a brand driven by passionate followers. "We wanted to try to understand what our consumers saw in us, so we looked at other brands where people were tattooing the logos on their bodies," he says. "The two that came to mind were Harley-Davidson and yoga. What we came up with is: it's a brand that can go into many other mediums but still preserve its identity."[2]

That sense of identity has made Zumba's success skyrocket. After starting out with just a website, videotape, and infomercial, the company went on to sell thousands of DVDs. Now classes are taught in more than 125 countries in 60,000-plus locations, with 12 million fans attending class each week. After their initial success in the infomercial arena, the owners were pondering what product should come next in order to expand the Zumba empire when the product found them. Fitness and dance instructors who had purchased the videotapes began calling in droves to ask how they could become certified in Zumba so they could teach it to their students.

Says Alberto Perlman, "We decided at that moment that our business was going to be about helping instructors become successful."[3] They held their initial training session in Miami with 150 participants and certified the first group of Zumba instructors. Although they had anticipated that the videos would be their major source of revenue, the desire for certification and community was so strong that the team created the Zumba Instructor Network, which has become an essential component of their business mix. By providing ongoing training and certification, as well as wholesale merchandise that instructors can resell to their students, the Zumba founders helped turn thousands of instructors—across the United States and from South Korea to Norway—into bona fide entrepreneurs.

In fact, growing the instructor and student base—with a goal of eventually reaching 100 million students—is the company's primary focus. With two investment firms now backing them, they've already expanded their brand into clothing and footwear and have launched a magazine called *ZLife*. And with hip-hop stars like Wyclef Jean and Pitbull and reggaeton singer Don Omar using Zumba to promote their music, it looks like entertainment may well be the company's future. "My dream is to see fitness concerts all over the world, traveling shows, permanent shows in Las Vegas," says Alberto Perlman. "The artists love it too, because it's a new way of selling their music."[4]

And yet, with all their big plans, what keeps the brand so competitive in a world where we've seen Jazzercise and Tae Bo all but disappear is that it is grounded in the promise of giving people a good time while they're getting fit. Says Perez, now officially dubbed the "chief creative officer," "Over the years, fitness became too complicated and difficult. The industry turned egocentric with an emphasis on instructors doing the exercises. It became a show. They forgot about normal people—mothers, grandmothers and the housewives who want to stay in shape and have some fun. That's the essence of Zumba."[5]

Even during the recession, the company continued to flourish, thanks in large part to its close relationship with its instructors, who have become the organization's biggest brand evangelists. States Perlman, "We create a platform to allow other people to be successful doing what they love, whether being successful means that you're losing weight or making money."[6] As long as Zumba Fitness keeps on building its distinctive "ditch the workout, join the party" platform, it's likely they will continue to samba their way to long-term success.

RELEVANCE AS COMPETITIVE EDGE

In his book *Brand Relevance: Making Competition Irrelevant*, David A. Aaker, professor emeritus of marketing strategy at UC–Berkeley's Haas School of Business, points out that brands that establish unique and relevant subcategories have a far better chance at success than those that try to go head-to-head with the category leaders.[7] Spending time trying to outsmart or outspend the competition is futile, Aaker suggests. "You can almost never change the competitive landscape by engaging in [it]," he states. But by carving out a smaller niche within a larger category and doing what the big guys do differently, innovative brands can create traction among consumers. This is precisely how Zumba found its foothold in the multi-billion-dollar fitness industry, establishing a subcategory so successful that it has become a category in itself.

Aaker advises that in order to identify opportunities in the marketplace, as well as prepare to face the competition, businesses need to ask themselves some key questions to get a better sense of their competitive position. These include:

1. **Is there a market for this concept?** The first step is to confirm that you've got a winner on your hands—or at least a shot at creating a significant customer base. Have you done your homework through consumer research, studying the current products and services in your space and testing the market to see whether you have a winning business offering?

2. **Can we compete and win?** Next, find out who the competition is and what they are doing in order to be successful. Is there room for someone new, different, or better in the space? Don't necessarily be put off by multiple competitors—this can often mean that there is consumer confusion and room

for someone who defines a strong niche brand (again, think *subcategory*) within the space.

3. **Do we need to be the market leader to be successful?** Determine whether it's imperative that your business be the first to market or the market leader in order to succeed. As Aaker points out, the iPod Nano wasn't the first of its kind, just the best. Tamara Monosoff of Mom Invented confirms that even if there are products or services in the market that serve a similar function, as long as you're not infringing on someone's copyright, then it can actually be easier to launch a business when a consumer need has already been established. Otherwise, you have to demonstrate that need and then educate your audience about it, which can often be an expensive and exhausting uphill battle.

Once you've evaluated the strength of your brand positioning—and this should be an ongoing process—you can begin to build the barriers that can kill, or at least forestall, the competition. While it may be impossible for you to compete with companies like Walmart or General Electric, which have the financial wherewithal to keep other companies at bay, if your brand is unique, relevant, and wildly appealing to your core customer—as Zumba is to its fun-loving fitness enthusiasts—you don't have to go head-to-head with the big guys. But you do have to differentiate yourself.

For most businesses, the smartest and most cost-effective way to create powerful marketplace differentiators in order to thwart the competition is to highlight the unique benefits of your business. If you're a small neighborhood retailer, for example, you can persuasively argue that you have deep roots in the community and can serve your clientele with customized service in a way that the big-box giants couldn't even attempt. You can also benefit from establishing a strong link between the overall category and your specific subcategory, such as nutrition and Whole Foods or fitness and Zumba. When you create a powerful connection between the category and your business, your customers will instantly think of you when they are looking for something in that space.

THE MANY FACES OF COMPETITION

While I believe that we live in a universe of abundant possibility, when I hear businesspeople proclaim that they have no competition, I think they are utterly naive and/or setting themselves up for failure.

We all have competition, and it comes in lots of forms. Although most people recognize *direct competition*—that is, those companies offering products and services that fill a similar need as theirs—they frequently underestimate the *indirect competition* and completely overlook the *invisible competition*. While direct competition to McDonald's would include Burger King and Arby's, indirect competitors could include everything from more people cooking at home to others going on a fast food–free diet—basically, anything that interferes with the customer wanting to buy your product because another option is preferable to them. Staying with the food metaphor for a moment, restaurants in completely different categories can also be indirect competitors. While the neighborhood pizza joint might not consider the sushi house a competitor, if it's down the street, in the same general price range, and looking for the same customers, it is indeed a competitor.

Invisible competitors are, by their nature, the most difficult ones to spot. These competitors don't look or feel like competition and may not be obvious at first glance but still somehow interfere with the prospect's decision to buy from you. It's worth developing a sort of branding sixth sense to see what might be up ahead in the marketplace that could potentially deter your clients from choosing you. Here are some things of which you should be mindful:

- **Customer fear.** We've all seen examples of prospects who get cold feet when faced with making a final buying decision. If this is happening to you on more than an occasional basis, you need to determine the root cause. Have you not sufficiently proven your value? Do you lack a solid guarantee that assuages their concerns? Are you failing to provide comparable case studies, client results, or references that would remove their purchase fear? (In my own experience, by the time prospects have reviewed the client testimonials on my website, they rarely request references or further proof of value. It's all out there for them to see.) It may be time to survey some trusted former customers to see whether you can figure out what's not working and correct it. *Recommendation: fix it fast.*

- **Unexpected alliances.** Sometimes your direct or indirect competitors unexpectedly join forces in ways that can challenge your business with a brutal one-two punch. For example, while carmakers are used to fighting against others in their class, imagine the increased competition that many faced when auto juggernauts Toyota and BMW announced their partnership to develop electric cars and a new sports vehicle. Being on the lookout for what might come to pass may seem a bit paranoid, but anything can happen—and often does—on our globally interconnected planet. *Recommendation: stay vigilant.*

- **New challengers.** Emerging companies, while nearly impossible to predict, always pose a threat to your business. By assuming that new competitors are out there—just ready to pounce on your customers—you'll stay value-driven and service-focused. *Recommendation: keep innovating.*

- **Fading relevance.** Sometimes companies (and, sadly, professionals) simply become irrelevant. While the FlipCam was a great product at a good price, once iPhone and others added HD video cameras—along with other features all in one smart phone—who needed an extra piece of hardware? You may not always be able to see around corners to predict what's coming next in terms of taste or technology, but regularly monitoring the competition and managing your own brand are the best ways to combat irrelevance. *Recommendation: be proactive.*

Here's an example of how competition sent what was once referred to as "the sport of kings," horse racing, into steady decline. When the Breeders' Cup, one of the world's biggest horse races along with the Kentucky Derby and the Dubai World Cup, recently took place at Southern California's Santa Anita Park, renowned race announcer Trevor Denman was there to call the race, just as he has been doing for three decades. Looking back to the early days of his 30-year career, Denman recalled, "The venue would easily get around 50,000 visitors on the weekends and 15,000 during the week. Now, it gets about 3,000 weekly visitors and about 10,000 on the weekends."[8]

But the drop-off wasn't due to direct competition from other horse races. It was due to indirect and invisible competition, which added up to produce its decreasing brand relevance. First of all, we're no longer a society in which horses are a primary mode of transportation or even a part of our daily lives, as they were even as late as the 1920s and '30s. As Denman told NPR rather wistfully, "Now it's only pony rides, and that's about it."[9] Add to this smaller presence the changed betting regulations and widespread use of the Internet. Now people don't need to go to the track to bet; they can simply click on their computer, place their wager online, and watch the race from the comfort of their own homes. While horse racing may have had its heyday, if you plan to outpace the direct, indirect, and invisible competition, it's critical that you identify and strengthen the unique factors that give your brand a competitive edge in the marketplace.

MINDSHARE MINUTE: IDENTIFY THE COMPETITION

Identify the competition to your business purpose by asking yourself the following questions:

1. Who is my direct competition—that is, those businesses or experts providing products or services similar to mine? What am I doing differently than those companies/ professionals? How can I better articulate those differentiators to my customers and prospects?

2. Who are the indirect competitors in my field? Identify those businesses whose offerings are not identical but might be seen to fulfill a similar need. How does the indirect competition stop potential customers from seeking me out? And how might I combat that?

3. Who are the invisible competitors that could challenge me? Imagine some scenarios in which inertia, fear, or competitive alliances might pose a threat to your business. How can you anticipate these challenges? What do you need to do to stay vigilant and ready to defend your brand?

OUT-COLLABORATING THE COMPETITION

"Collaboration is our competitive edge," says John Sullivan, senior director of strategies and effectiveness for Kao USA, the U.S. subsidiary of Kao Brands. While you may not have heard of Kao, you have most certainly heard of their health and beauty products for women, including Ban, John Frieda, Jergens, Curel, and Biore. A relatively small player in the industry, with only about 4.5 percent of market share, Kao is dwarfed in comparison to consumer products giants like Procter & Gamble, Unilever, L'Oreal, and Johnson & Johnson—which is why they've determined that out-collaborating the competition is essential to their success.[10]

"We're fighting huge competitors," says Karen Frank, vice president of marketing for Kao USA. "We're clearly the underdogs. But underdogs do win." Frank backs up her claim by citing the work of Ivan Arreguin-Toft, an international security expert and authority in *asymmetric conflict*. Asymmetric conflict is a conflict, war, or insurrection in which the warring parties differ significantly in military size and/or capabilities.[11]

In his publication *How the Weak Win Wars: A Theory of Asymmetric Conflict*, Dr. Arreguin-Toft cites the Muhammad Ali–George Foreman "Rumble in the Jungle" as a seminal example of the ostensibly weaker participant besting the stronger party.[12] In what was expected to be a knockout by Foreman by round three, Muhammad Ali instead lured his opponent to the ropes in round two, taunting him repeatedly until Foreman lost his composure and pounded him against the ropes. What is now known as the *rope-a-dope* strategy worked wonders, and Foreman exhausted himself, while the ropes took the brunt of his punches, instead of Ali. Ali knocked him out in the eighth round, making boxing history. According to Arreguin-Toft, this is an example of a weaker opponent using strategy rather than might to overpower a stronger one. If power were always the deciding factor, the strong would win every time. But strategy is often just as important, if not more so.

Although an earlier theory suggested that the weaker players in a conflict have more at stake—that is, their lives depend on victory, and they are therefore more motivated to win—this hypothesis has been shown to be false or at least questionable. What Arreguin-Toft, then a postdoctoral candidate at Harvard and now a professor at Boston University, discovered in his study of 200 years of conflict is:

- "Weaker" players are victorious in nearly 30 percent of all asymmetric conflicts.
- Weaker players win with increasing frequency over time.
- Strategy, rather than strength, allows weaker players to win uneven battles.
- Understanding your opponent's strategy and developing a counterstrategy is critical to underdog success.

Frank, a veteran of Procter & Gamble as well as a former entrepreneur, is passionate about providing the Kao team with the tools and tactics to win market share. She has developed an entire program around what she calls *underdog marketing*, and she even went so far as to trademark the term, probably a wise precaution in an industry that loves to imitate. As elegant herself as the beauty products she represents, Frank nonetheless displays the focus and drive of a general as she outlines her marketing plan for the Kao USA sales team. Posing a question at a Kao sales conference that is at once a challenge and a rallying cry, Frank asks the crowd, "So *how* are we going to win?"

Cautioning the group that the relationship with the consumer must be kept top of mind at all times, she reminds them that they must maintain a holistic view of the customer rather than succumb to stereotypes. That holistic view should include what Frank calls "the boomer consumer," that is, the older woman who isn't old but is confident and attractive and has a high level of discretionary income and a presence on social media. "The myths aren't true," she tells the sales team, meaning that not everything has to be about gorgeous twentysomething women but should include women of different ages, skin color, needs, and preferences.

Unveiling her strategy, Frank outlines five principles of Underdog Marketing:

- Change the way the game is played.
- Focus on and exploit unique strengths.
- Bring extreme focus and simplicity to the message.
- Bring unconventional thinking to the table.
- Leverage partner relationships.

As an example of "changing the way the game is played," Frank told me about an unconventional marketing ploy her team tried with Biore, the facial cleansing strips. Since the brand was favored by young adults for its pore-cleaning powers, one of Frank's staff members suggested they try a radio campaign to reach that audience. None of the bigger brands was using radio for facial products on the assumption that the customer needed to *see* the face on TV or in a print ad. The Kao team tried the strategy out in a couple of test markets, using the deejays as endorsers. The spots were so successful that they kicked off a national radio campaign on rock and indie stations—reaching exactly the right audience for Biore. By bucking conventional wisdom (that is, that facial products require a visual medium for promotion) and taking a calculated risk when results could be easily measured before making a sizable investment, Kao scored a big win. The takeaway for you? Go where your customer is but your competition isn't.

In an industry that thrives on copycatting, Frank and the entire Kao team have learned to be watchful of what the competition is doing. In fact, the Kao-owned John Frieda Hair Care line was the originator of anti-frizz hair products, which were so successful that they were almost immediately imitated by most of the major brands. Hyper-aware of what the big competitor brands are doing, Frank also keeps an eye on smaller players to see how they've broken through to reach their audience.

Organix Hair Care changed the game for themselves and found a market niche by creating a different kind of experience for the consumer. Using what Frank calls "romantic ingredients," such as macadamia oil, bamboo extract, and ginger, and brightly colored packaging that stands out on the shelf, Organix has created what looks and feels like a luxury product but comes at a drugstore price. By finding a unique niche—right down to the scent, colors, and packaging—Organix has created a subcategory brand with staying power.

Another fast-growing skincare competitor, Cetaphil demonstrates the underdog principle of leveraging relationships. Its cleansers and moisturizers are recommended by more dermatologists and pediatricians than any other brand, signaling to consumers—especially moms—that they can be trusted.

So what does asymmetric battle theory have to do with you and your brand? While I won't go quite so far as to say "it's a war out there," competition is real and often fierce. Watching the competition and being able to anticipate its moves can help you determine your own—which takes us back to Sullivan's point about collaboration giving Kao a competitive edge. While the Kao team may not be able to outman or outspend the giants in health and beauty products, they can definitely out-collaborate them.

Sullivan says that Kao uses its smaller size to its advantage. By encouraging timely and transparent communication, the company doesn't suffer from a lot of internal politics. People are honest and straightforward, and although there's little finger-pointing, they don't hesitate to put issues on the table and get to the bottom of problems. "When we recruit," he states, "we typically screen for whether or not someone is truly a team player by designing questions that peel back the layers." By creating a culture and not a bureaucracy, Kao has developed a workforce of bold-spirited, passionate people who work well together and aren't afraid to take chances. "What are we good at?" Sullivan asks and then answers, "Customer service, on-time delivery, having products people respond to, and bringing the right people to the right meetings." As if it weren't already abundantly clear, Sullivan sums it all up by saying, "Negativity doesn't fly."[13]

GO BOLD OR GO HOME

Edgy. Provocative. Badass. These adjectives are just a few used to describe the bold online clothing brand Nasty Gal, founded by 28-year-old Sophia Amoruso. She doesn't much care if the name offends. As she told *Forbes* magazine in an interview about her meteoric rise, "If it's a big shock when you hear it, you're probably not our customer anyway."[14] A community college dropout with no business or fashion background, Amoruso can afford to offend a few people. According to *Inc.* magazine, Nasty Gal—with its 10,160 percent growth from 2008 to 2011—is the fastest-growing company in Los Angeles and the fastest-growing retail company period.[15]

The company began as an eBay store that Amoruso ran out of her bedroom. She'd spend hours searching thrift shops, vintage stores, and flea markets, looking for great bargains among the junk; once she even found a Chanel jacket for which she paid $8 at Salvation Army and resold for $1,050. She was so successful with her eBay store that she began promoting her own site,

NastyGalVintage.com, until the "nasty" URL got her kicked off eBay.

Eventually adding non-vintage clothing to the mix, the self-taught Amoruso bootstrapped the business, funding it herself as she sourced the products, took the photographs, and even packed and shipped the clothing. When the business really began to take off, she moved to Los Angeles to be closer to her vendors, a potential employee pool, and the aesthetic vibe she wanted for the company. After British venture capital firm Index Ventures supplied the company with $9 million in a first round of funding, they came back just five months later as NastyGal's sole investors, with a second investment of $40 million.

So what sets Amoruso and Nasty Gal apart from all the other clothiers—off- and online? According to Deborah Benton, who left Kim Kardashian's ShoeDazzle to become Nasty Gal's president and chief operating officer, "There's not an ounce of pretension about her. That core value of authenticity—it comes through loud and clear in the brand."[16] Audacity seems to be Amoruso's particular brand of authenticity, and it's one that resonates with the company's loyal fans, who can't seem to get enough of Nasty Gal. With a core audience of 250,000 shoppers, mostly women ages 18 to 24, more than a quarter visit the site once a day for approximately seven minutes. The top 10 percent of fans—that is, 25,000 people—visit the site more than 100 times per month.

Amoruso's own style gives Nasty Gal its, well, nastiness. Named for a 1975 album by funk blues singer Betty Davis (the second wife of Miles Davis), Amoruso credits Davis as the "patron saint of badass women" on the company website. Amoruso's own unabashedly sexy style—mixing platform boots, leather miniskirts, and tie-dyed halter tops—is a hit with young women who want a high-fashion look that feels more East Village than Wall Street. Even female fans in fairly conservative professions have discovered that, if done judiciously, they can successfully mix a Nasty Gal piece or two in with their career clothes.

But it was Amoruso's skillful use of social media that brought her to the attention of Index Ventures. Initially learning the ropes on MySpace, she now has more than 494,000 Facebook likes, 365,000 Instagram followers, and 60,000 Twitter followers as of the writing of this book. By feeding that loyal group of young fans—who fall right into the sweet spot of daily social media usage—Nasty Gal's customer base continues to grow. Also attractive to her investors, most items on the site are under $100, with a 60 percent profit margin, primarily because Nasty Gal sticks to a straight-pricing model rather than offering discounts, daily deals, or promo codes.

The message is clear: Amoruso's edgy taste, the quality of the products, her ability to engage loyal fans, and a no-nonsense business model have made Nasty Gal a winner in the competitive and often fickle world of fashion. Now, with the influx of cash from Index, she is launching her own collection, Weird Science, a nod to technology. Up until now, Nasty Gal has relied on vintage clothing or products from a handful of vendors including UNIF and Shakuhachi, but now she'll be releasing her own line of tops, pants, dresses, sweaters, and denim, with a starting price of $68. A bonus for Los Angeles: all of her clothing will be made locally. Further expanding the edgy brand, Amoruso will be launching a lifestyle magazine, *Super Nasty*, which will be included free in customer shipments and will feature spreads on fashion, music, and culture. If she does it right—and she hasn't made many missteps so far, despite her age and relative inexperience—Nasty Gal may be yet another example, like Zumba and Harley-Davidson, of a brand that can extend into multiple arenas but maintain its core identity with its passionate followers.

BRAND BUILDING BLOCK #4: DEVELOPING YOUR ONLINE BRAND

While it's clear that delivering authentic value to your core customer consistently over time must be the foundation of your brand, in order to compete, you have to be able to articulate abstract concepts in ways that make them concrete for your buyers. And while there's more to your brand than merely having a cool website, catchy slogan, and some social media messages, you need all those brand expressions to help you grab and hold your customers' attention, especially in our attention-challenged society.

THIS BUD'S FOR YOU: COMPANY SLOGANS

As we've already seen, brevity can be a significant key to stickiness, and therefore company slogans are one of the more powerful ways to communicate brand essence in shorthand. But why do some slogans, such as Wendy's "Where's the Beef?" or L'Oreal's "Because You're Worth It," become part of our long-term lexicon whereas others fade into oblivion or go utterly unnoticed right from the start? How do graphics support or detract from slogans? And how do we use that magic combo of words and pictures to beat the competition and plant our brand firmly in the minds of the public?

As much art as science, the best slogans sum up your brand promise and business personality all in one sticky little catchphrase that, try as they might, your customers can't seem to get out of their heads and your competitors can't seem to surpass. As important as your company name and graphic logo, your tagline is one of those touchstones that helps people remember that you're out there, just waiting to do business with them. So what makes one slogan memorable and another mediocre? Let's dissect some of the all-time great taglines and see what makes them work.

- **Memorability.** There are a number of ways to get your message to stick. As we discovered in Chapter One, engaging all the senses is a powerful way to convey a message. So while the wording of the tagline for the Energizer bunny keeps "going and going and going," we also get the image of the bunny and the sound of the clanging cymbals to drive home the message. It may be annoying, but it's memorable.

- **Powerful promise.** One of the all-time great examples is the classic FedEx slogan, "When it absolutely positively has to be there overnight." Notice FedEx didn't claim to be the *only* carrier that could deliver your package to its destination overnight, just the only one you could actually depend upon to keep its promise. Read their slogan out loud and notice the rhythm and musicality of the language. With its punchy staccato tempo, you practically want to tap dance to the sound.

- **Call-to-action.** Nike's spot-on and much-cited "Just Do It" sums up the energy of the brand and raises a call-to-action at the same time. Not only does the slogan capture the take-no-prisoners attitude of the company, but it connects directly to exercise and athleticism with its "no excuses" message. It almost screams at us, "Put on the shoes and run, darn it." Add the visual element of the famous "Nike Swoosh," with its distinct feeling of motion, and you've got an action-packed, multi-sensory slogan.

- **Sex appeal.** A master at using sex to sell everything from underwear to blue jeans, Calvin Klein's tagline for the fragrance Obsession is about as close to poetry as taglines get. Love it or hate it, "Between love and madness lies Obsession" sends the senses reeling with possibility. Notice the rolling sound of the O vowels and the lush alliteration of the two Ls.

How do you create a slogan that captures that essence of your business while differentiating you from the competition? First of all, consider your audience. What is the problem you solve and the promise you've made to them? Next, what is the tone and style that feels authentic to you and will best reflect your business personality? Are you edgy, snarky, conservative, patriotic, funny, or comforting? Start with the promise and the personality and jot down as many adjectives as come to mind.

A great goal is to create a clear, simple message of seven words or less. If you can be clear and clever, that's terrific. If you can only be one or the other, clarity trumps cleverness every time. But don't expect a great slogan to materialize overnight. Crafting a slogan takes work, creativity, and craftsmanship. You may want to gather a group for a brainstorming session, starting with a handful of adjectives and then letting everyone riff on the theme. I find it most effective to get the group started together and then split up to work solo. Reconvene later after each person has had time to come up with his own list, swapping ideas and sharing reactions. Let your combined list sit for a few days and then poll the gang for each person's top-five favorites.

Depending upon your budget, of course, you can also hire a professional copywriter, marketing or advertising agency, or online slogan shop to help you. Once you've got your tagline, use it in multiple ways to reinforce your message, such as on your website, social media, advertising, marketing materials, and business cards. Just don't get too locked in, since it will more than likely evolve along with your brand.

MINDSHARE MINUTE: CREATING YOUR STICKY TAGLINE

Go to www.LibbyGill.com for a Creating Your Sticky Taglines worksheet, including a list of all-time favorite slogans.

CONNECTIONS THAT BEAT THE COMPETITION

Armed with a website that reflects your authentic business personality (as discussed in Chapter Four) and succinct messaging that sums up your brand promise in one pithy statement, it's time to dive into the online world. Even if your business isn't conducted primarily on the Internet like Nasty Gal's, every professional—including those in the corporate world—needs an online image in order to communicate and compete. Plenty of books deal with the mechanics of how to create an effective Facebook page, a robust Twitter following, and lots of quality LinkedIn connections—and I encourage you to read them. But what I want to deal with here is how you capture the essence of your brand online—given the Internet's unique constraints—in order to engage customers and keep the competition at bay.

When you think of social media as an opportunity to differentiate yourself in the marketplace as you contribute value, information, education, or perspective—rather than a chance to sell—it completely changes your strategic approach to competing online. Determining the best and highest use of social media for connecting with your customers can also help you prioritize and prevent the time-suck challenges that online platforms present if left unchecked.

Once you are clear on the differentiators that help you connect to your ideal customers, think about how your message translates to different online platforms. Be aware that each platform has a different structure and tone and that you'll need to customize your communications accordingly. Managing a social media strategy takes time and effort, so you want to focus on the platforms that best extend your message. Most of all, remember that social media is based on communicating and sharing, not constant self-promotion or blatant advertising. Using social media for business is about getting people to like, know, and trust you. The more you engage in a two-way dialogue, the more people will come to rely on your brand.

If you're in a corporate structure, make sure that everyone understands the brand story and knows how to customize the message to fit the style of the online platform, as well as meet their customers' needs. For example, your head of sales or marketing could be writing blog posts aimed at customers while your human resources team is communicating a message intended to recruit new professionals to the company. While you may be providing content for different audience segments, the overall brand story should always remain constant and cohesive. Provide training to anyone who will be using social media to connect with internal or external customers, clarifying the overall brand story as well as specific message points appropriate for the audience. The more consistent you are with your message, the more competitive you'll be.

If you have a team, divide and conquer by aligning people's strengths with platforms that are the best fit for them—but be sure to take a holistic approach to creating a brand presence that makes sense across multiple platforms. For most businesses, your website will be the mothership of your brand, the central hub to which all your social media platforms connect. You may want to consider using some or all of the following social media platforms as opportunities to connect with your customers and create ongoing value:

- **Facebook.** Create a company, group, and/or fan page to tap into the site's more than one billion users, half of whom check their Facebook pages on mobile devices.
- **Twitter.** Great for short, humorous posts and quick hits of information.
- **YouTube.** One of the most personal ways you can engage your customers because the videos allow them to look you in the eye—at least virtually.
- **LinkedIn.** The best professional online network for creating a presence for your company principals and key executives.
- **Pinterest and Instagram.** Some of the fastest-growing sites; they are especially relevant if you work in a visual medium like fashion or interior decorating and/or if you're trying to reach women.
- **Blogs and guest blogs.** Host your own blog for longer informational pieces and ongoing communications and/or contribute regularly to other expert blogs to get in front of new customers.

- **Syndicated articles.** Use online tools like ezinearticles.com, goarticles.com, or articlesgalley.com for article syndication to get your name to a broader base.

Although it's great to let your employees' humor, expertise, and personality shine through their posts, don't let anyone stray too far from the core message, raise negatives without prior guidance, or give away proprietary information. Online communication is instantaneous and lasting, so make sure you schedule plenty of training time, approve posts in advance, and monitor your messaging on a daily basis. The following are some tips for creating an effective social media process:

- **Stay brand true.** Make sure that everyone who is involved in implementing social media messaging is consistent in tone, type of value provided, and graphic usage. Although every platform is different and the look and feel in terms of both language and graphics will need to be customized for each platform, the customer should always know that he or she is on a platform related to your business. Continuous use of the logo, tagline, and core messages are critical to this effort.
- **Define the mission for each platform.** Each platform has a different language, tone, and purpose. You need to create a vision and business objectives for each platform.
- **Manage mistakes.** If someone provides misinformation, correcting it quickly and transparently is the best course of action. How you handle mistakes online gives your customers a great sense of how you handle them in the rest of your business.
- **Create a social media calendar.** Determine how often and what kinds of content you will be posting on each of your

social media platforms. You'll want a mix of evergreen messages (that is, those that will stay fresh and can be posted at any time) and those that are time and date sensitive, such as updates from the company or industry.

- **Create great content.** By giving great value to your customers, you will create an ongoing dialogue and sense of loyalty. The more your community gets to know, like, and trust you, the more likely they are to buy from you. You can also offer incentives such as promo codes, special discounts, and contests to create buzz and excitement. Just don't overdo it.

- **Cross-promote across sites.** Be sure to cross-promote across your social media platforms, letting your Twitter followers know to check out a longer piece on Facebook or sending your Facebook followers to YouTube to check out a new video post. That way, people will begin to become familiar with your network of sites. By having a cohesive but customized look for each site, people will be able to find and interact with your company in multiple ways.

- **Respond, respond, respond.** Make sure you respond to comments and posts, especially any negative ones. Social media is meant for two-way engagement, and your audience will become annoyed if you only post and never respond. Ask questions, pose issues, start a conversation, and be sure to check in and respond on a regular basis.

- **Keep up the momentum.** Once you begin a comprehensive social media strategy, do not abandon your efforts. It's easy to decide that "it's not working" or you can't see the results fast enough. It takes time and experimentation to build a loyal following. Don't leave people hanging once you get them interested.

- **Measure success.** Be sure to measure success by checking your analytics regularly to see what clicks with your audience. It is only by learning what is of most value to them that you will be able to build your following. Keep tweaking your editorial calendar and content to make sure your posts are timely, brief, and relevant.
- **Finally, follow the rules of "netiquette."** If you wouldn't say or do it in the real world, or if you wouldn't want your mother to read it, don't do or say it online. That goes for employees' personal social media as well. Even when off the clock, they still represent the company and should act accordingly.

MONITOR THE COMPETITION WHILE YOU MANAGE YOUR BRAND

In the 1977 movie *Annie Hall*, Woody Allen's alter ego Alvy Singer compares a relationship to a shark, saying, "If it doesn't constantly move forward, it dies. What we've got on our hands is a dead shark." Brands are a lot like that. If they're not constantly moving forward, they die—or at least they risk losing significant market share. Even though change is scary—for both companies and customers—your brand should be in a state of constant evolution. Not revolution, mind you, although sometimes that's necessary too. Rather, by being in a state of continual watchfulness, you can manage your brand, make course corrections, and monitor the competition at the same time. That's the only way to stay ahead of the curve and keep your brand relevant to returning and new customers.

YOU SAY YOU WANT AN EVOLUTION

Harley-Davidson, with its more than 100 years of history, is an expert at evolving its brand. Since selling its first bike in the early

1900s, Harleys have become known for their heavy weight, distinctive throaty engine roar, and appeal to long-distance highway riders. Weathering wars, depressions, and a public image as the scourge of the suburbs, Harley has learned to change with the changing times. Nonetheless, some critics say their time has come—and gone.[17]

Harley-Davidson detractors suggest that the company has ridden the wave of baby boomers—the largest generational category in our current economy—and that wave is about to crest. Fueled by a desire to escape the blandness of the suburbs while hanging onto their youth, boomers sent Harley sales to an all-time high in 2006, only to crash, along with the rest of the economy, in 2009. It's arguable as to whether sales have slumped because aging boomers are now full-time retirees sticking closer to home or because the bikes, at approximately $20,000, are luxury items in a time when most people don't have that kind of discretionary income.

But Harley is not waiting around to find out. As the economy shakes out and the boomers get grayer, the company has turned its focus to building new markets, adding women, minorities, and novice riders to the mix. So far, the strategy is working. Women riders now account for nearly 11 percent of sales, up from 5 percent just ten years ago. By courting women through clubs, female-oriented "garage parties," instructional classes, and videos—like one that shows women how to pick up a 500-pound fallen motorcycle without getting injured—the company has eradicated the badass biker chick stereotype.[18] They've also eliminated the woman-as-passive-passenger image, in which the gal on the back of the bike hangs onto her man for dear life. By giving women the keys—literally—the company has made Harley attractive to a more mainstream (and bigger) female audience.

With its ongoing neighborhood events, clubs, and races, Harley has also made a concerted effort to get more young people hooked on riding. Their website boldly proclaims, "Now Recruiting Future Riders," and offers classes for "anyone ready to ride," code for new customers. As one good-looking young guy of about 30—a coveted demographic—says gleefully on a video on the Harley-Davidson website, "I don't know much about bikes yet, but that's why I'm here and after tonight that will all be changed."[19]

At the risk of looking a little long in the tooth, just like its base of boomer riders, Harley is still courting the seniors. And as many of them are installing handrails in their showers for increased stability, Harley is providing better balance—for their P&L sheets as well as their riders—by pushing sales of their three-wheeled trikes. Many older riders who are dealing with weakened muscles, knee or back injuries, and fading eyesight have abandoned their freewheeling Hogs for the steadier three-wheelers. With cushier seats and a trunk for storage, the trikes' popularity started with do-it-yourself expansion kits that converted two-wheelers into three-wheeled machines. Today, Harley has a full range of already-assembled trikes, starting at a pricey $30,000.[20]

Like Zumba and Nasty Gal, Harley-Davidson has built a community based on the passion of its loyal followers. Although critics may wonder whether trikes can help the company and its fans recapture their fading youth, I wouldn't count Harley out just yet. Let's give them another century or so.

REPUTATION MATTERS

Along with a 24/7 news cycle and easy online shopping, the Internet has given a voice to the masses. No longer does a disgruntled customer send a letter of complaint to the manager of a business, hoping for a response. Today, if you're not happy with something, you can publicly say so, reaching millions via Yelp, TripAdvisor, or

Facebook. So it's more important than ever that we pay attention to our reputation. And while we're monitoring what our customers are saying about us, it's just one more step to check out the latest word on the competition.

For the past 13 years, Harris Interactive has conducted the Harris Poll Reputation Quotient (RQ) study, asking the general public to measure the reputations of the 60 most visible companies in the country, using six different metrics.[21] While traditional manufacturing companies have tended to score well in the past, companies that combine multiple industries and are perceived to have strong leaders fared the best in the 2012 poll. Not surprisingly, given recent history, financial institutions and oil companies slipped down the list. The five top-scoring companies were Apple, Google, Coca-Cola, Amazon.com, and Kraft Foods.

"We are seeing the emergence of a group of companies that garner reputation equity by being positively associated with multiple industries," says Robert Fronk, executive vice president and Global Corporate Reputation Practice Lead for Harris Interactive. "Companies like Apple, Google, and Amazon.com combine innovation and leadership across multiple business areas, giving them true competitive advantage."[22]

The poll measures six key dimensions, outlined in the following, along with the top-scoring company in each area:

- Social responsibility—Whole Foods
- Emotional appeal—Amazon.com
- Financial performance—Apple
- Products & services—Apple
- Vision & leadership—Apple
- Workplace environment—Apple

Even if you're not among the top 60 most visible companies, it's easier than you think—and critically important—to monitor your reputation as well as that of the competition. After all, only by knowing when they're zigging will you know it's time to zag. And while technology has made us more vulnerable to customer complaints, it's also given us some powerful reputation management techniques. Here are some tools you can utilize to keep an eye on your own image while also keeping an eye on the competition:

- **Google Alerts.** Register a keyword or phrase and get an email whenever it appears online.
- **Yext Rep.** Track mentions and reviews of your business on social media sites such as Facebook, Twitter, Yelp, and Foursquare.
- **Google Analytics.** Track your web traffic, including how visitors come to and use your website. Also analyze marketing results and sales conversion.
- **Viralheat.** Manage your social media platforms, monitor customer engagement, and schedule posts from one dashboard.
- **Trackur.** Monitor your online reputation, as well as news mentions and PR campaigns. Use their tracking software to follow your employees or competition.

CAPTURE THE MINDSHARE SNAPSHOT: COMMUNICATING YOUR COMPETITIVE EDGE

Once you've clarified your marketplace value, identified the differentiators that set you apart from others in your industry, and created a strategy that gives you a competitive edge, it's time to communicate that message to your team (even if your team is just you). As we've seen, brevity and focus are critical to getting that message across.

CHALLENGE

When veteran sales strategist Paul Nunnari joined Kao USA after a successful tenure at Procter & Gamble, he saw that there was something special about the Kao culture. Despite formidable competition, he recognized the workforce's dogged determination to be the best in the business. To articulate and share Kao's uniqueness—in a very Kao-esque collaboration—Nunnari pulled together a task force from the sales, marketing, marketing services, finance, and human resources teams to hammer out a value statement that became known as the Kao Kurrency.

TACTICS

With the goal of developing a value statement that anyone at Kao could use to build partnerships and leverage resources, Nunnari's team came up with the "3 Pillars of Kao Kurrency." Those pillars are:

- **Superior customer service.** Kao reps, including those in high-level leadership positions, regularly make the rounds from retailers to supply chain managers to not only look for areas of improvement but also thank the people who are working so hard to make Kao a better company.
- **Portfolio leadership.** Kao provides ongoing thought leadership and education to its partners so they understand how to position their "problem solution brands."

They are experts in their category, with products created by professional stylists and salon owners. By knowing what retailers need—sometimes before they do—they are always ready to provide shopper and consumer studies, screenings, and training to their partners.

- **Performance partnership.** With a small team and limited resources, the Kao team does their homework before placing a bet. With every decision, they think about where they're going to get the biggest bang for their buck. Often the strategy and creativity, rather than mere dollars, get the best ROI. But this approach requires rigor and scrutiny in evaluating the market, measuring success, and continuing improvement—all standard at Kao USA.[23]

MORE

Create a competition-busting customer service promise for your company. Visit www.LibbyGill.com for a Creating Your Customer Currency Statement worksheet.

Chapter Six

COMMUNICATE

"Talking Your Walk" to Influence and Inspire

The single biggest problem in communication is the illusion that it has taken place.

—*George Bernard Shaw*

WHEN PASADENA-BASED HEATHER RIM ATTEMPTS TO EXPLAIN her decision to leave Disney for a job at manufacturing firm Avery Dennison, she is frequently greeted with raised eyebrows. Why, people want to know, would she leave a global entertainment company featuring movies, theme parks, and television shows—not to mention Mickey Mouse—to work for a company best known for making sticky labels?

Beside the fact that Avery Dennison is a Fortune 500 company with 30,000 employees working in 60 countries around the world, the reason was simple. As a marketing and communications expert, Rim jumped at the opportunity to help rebrand a nearly 100-year-old organization with multiple business lines including pressure-sensitive materials used in everything from transportation to health care, retail branding and information management systems, and specialty adhesive materials. And, yes, sticky labels.

Ironically, when Rim—now vice president of Global Corporate Communications (GCC)—first joined the company, she discovered that when employees were asked how they would describe Avery Dennison to friends, the majority responded, "We make labels." It made little difference that the office products division accounted for only 14 percent of the company's assets. It was apparently easier for people to point to the consumer-facing part of the company than to describe the disparate branding and technology solutions that they provided to customers throughout the world.[1]

For Rim, the opportunity to have an impact on the brand was a big part of the attraction. Her call-to-action for the communications team was to connect the dots across the organization and create an employer brand that celebrated Avery Dennison's collegial culture and innovative products. Since most of the company was focused on business-to-business activities, she planned to elevate the brand to give the employees a more accurate and descriptive company story to tell; inspire top talent to come aboard; and create a compelling message that would stick, if you will, with Avery's external customers.

WE GIVE YOU A WORLD TO WORK WITH

When I first met Rim a couple of years ago, her group had been newly reorganized and she'd taken on some social media and corporate philanthropy duties in addition to her role as head of the corporate communications team. Many of her team members had overlapping responsibilities yet had never met face to face, so she decided to fly them in from around the world for a summit. I was the facilitator for several days as Rim and her group hashed out some big questions: What is the Avery Dennison brand? How do we communicate this brand effectively both internally and externally? What is the communications team's brand within the greater corporate brand? For a company that manufactures products as far ranging as the clothing labels you'd find in the lining of your favorite suit to the adhesive materials used in wound dressings and the reflective surfaces on road signs, answering this set of questions was a pretty tall order.

When Rim and I caught up again recently, her team's rebranding efforts had been so successful that she had just been asked to deliver a presentation to a group of corporate executives from other Fortune 500 companies. Her colleagues were eager to hear her thoughts about challenging conventional wisdom and finding easy-to-employ solutions to break through barriers and longstanding (some might even say "old school") traditions that would prevent them from being able to effect change in a meaningful way. As Heather diplomatically put it, "A lot of companies have very deep roots, and introducing new ways of thinking can be like trying to turn a ship around. Avery Dennison is a 77-year-old company, so being able to help take it into the next phase of its journey using simple, inexpensive solutions got people pretty excited."

Like other companies that survived the economic downturn of 2008–2010, Avery Dennison wasn't interested in fancy research or expensive long-term consulting solutions to refocus their branding efforts. Rim was called upon to deliver thoughtful, cost-effective strategies that made bottom-line sense.

Fortunately, many of her team's efforts can be duplicated and scaled by companies with more modest budgets and limited manpower. From my own background leading public relations departments for entertainment studios, I know firsthand that a creative communications effort, strategically conceived and aggressively enacted, can often be as effective as a big bucks marketing campaign. Why? Because the public—and, more specifically, your customer—has become sophisticated, even jaded, about marketing and can sniff out a paid promotion a mile away, even when it comes in a clever "advertorial" package. However, most people are far less skeptical of legitimate editorial coverage in a trusted newspaper, magazine, television, or radio outlets or in peer reviews like you'd see on Yelp or Angie's List. Third-party endorsement from a reliable source can be the critical influencer that drives buying decisions when it comes to choosing a hairstylist, home computer, or health care provider. The same is true internally: employees are looking for straightforward communications and authentic leadership. They know BS when they hear it too.

As we've seen with companies like Cabela's, the most effective communicators listen first and talk second. Cabela's built their Nature of Cabela's program based on employee beliefs and values, put powerful language that resonated with their workforce into the Cabela's Field Guide, and then rolled out the program with care and proper training. The result was millions of dollars in sales. In a similar process, Rim's team "listened in" via employee engagement surveys, interviews, and group forums. They learned that their workforce was proud of the fact that they were surrounded by Avery Dennison products in their everyday lives, just like their customers were. Building on this idea, the communications team refined the brand story to a message of "We give you a world to work with."

As Rim observes:

> Ultimately, our employer brand reinforces the idea that opportunity is everywhere. After the research we did talking to employees about why they were excited to come work at Avery Dennison, why they stay, why they refer friends, and why they're so proud to be part of this company, it's because of this world of possibilities and connections that they have. People really like the fact that, at any given time, they can be on a call with people from 10 different countries speaking 15 different languages. A lot of companies say they have a global presence, and maybe once a month you'll be on a call with someone from another country. But here, whether it's online or in person, people are looking at how they can leverage the global footprint we have.

Telling the right story—that is, one that is as authentic as it is compelling—is the critical starting point for effective communication.

BRAND BUILDING BLOCK #5: CREATING YOUR BRAND'S STORY, STYLE, AND STRUCTURE

By having a well-defined communications process in place—before you need it—you put yourself in a *proactive* rather than a *reactive* position in which you're not just dealing with problems as they arise. Instead, by having a structured program grounded in strategy, as well as trained personnel to manage the process, you're always ready to articulate your brand positively, as well as deal with the negatives when necessary.

Every business, regardless of size, needs to consider the following three key elements when creating their internal and external communications processes:

1. Know the brand story you want to tell, as well as the key messages that support and further the story without diluting its primary theme. This includes not only being able to articulate the core brand story that explains your purpose and promise but also having supporting messages that can be tailored for specific situations, from product launches to crisis management. While the supporting messages will change according to the circumstances, the core brand story will essentially remain the same.

2. It's important that you establish a tone for your brand messaging that accurately reflects your business personality and resonates with your core customer. Whether you're a rock-solid neighbor like State Farm or a luxurious ocean-liner like Crystal Cruises, your overall style will stay the same, with only minor variations made to suit specific events. Consider, for example, how differently

State Farm and Crystal Cruises might frame a call-to-action for a limited-time special offer. State Farm would probably tell you something like, "There's no better time than right now to protect your home and family," while Crystal might suggest, "Experience ever-changing views and unparalleled luxury with our special book-now fares."

3. Finally, you'll need to have a structure in place for dealing with ongoing communication, as well as situational issues ranging from positive ones like announcing expansion plans to negative ones like workplace accidents. By having a communications protocol as well as necessary materials in place, you won't be forced to scramble for data or approvals at the last minute. Your communications program should include editorial calendars, approval processes, and standardized brand language. It should address all of your communications vehicles, such as your website, blogs, press releases, and traditional and social media.

The communications team at Avery Dennison uses a clever acronym called *Magic T* as a review guide each time they begin a new process. As Rim explains it, *Magic T* is an easy-to-remember phrase that helps the staff think through the entire strategy whenever they begin a campaign or interview process, thereby ensuring that they have a strong foundation on which to build. Here's what *Magic T* stands for:

- **M—Message.** What are the top three things you want people to do/know/remember?

- **A—Audience.** Who are your audiences?
- **G—Goal.** What are you trying to accomplish with the program?
- **I—Issues.** What are the issues and/or questions that you anticipate or that might impact the program?
- **C—Channels.** Which communication channels or vehicles are appropriate and optimal for each audience?
- **T—Timing.** When are the critical deadlines/milestones that need to be targeted?

YOUR BRAND STORY: ONCE MORE WITH FEELING

While we'll continue to address how you define your authentic brand throughout this book, it's well worth it to dive a little deeper into how you articulate your brand story through your communications. As we've seen, brands that evoke emotions are more likely to get our attention than those that don't. When brand messages bypass our logical brains and hook us on an emotional level, it can be the start of a connection that leads us to want to learn more. When our subsequent experience with those products or services speaks to our personal values and exceeds our expectations, it can be the start of long-term brand loyalty.

The quality and frequency of customer communications can have a huge impact on building that consumer relationship. Some companies are so adept at communicating a message that reflects their unique purpose while reminding people of their product that it's almost as though they have created a brand language all their own, a language that they've taught us to speak along with them. And while one slogan, ad, commercial, or newsletter will rarely make or break a company, an ongoing series of cohesive messages customized for specific platforms—that evolve with changing tastes and needs—can keep customers connected for years. Just think about mega-brander Coca-Cola and the commercials you saw growing up. In 1954 that message was "For People on the Go," in 1970 it was "It's the Real Thing," and in 2012 it was "Open Happiness." Then, of course, there were also the truly groundbreaking ads, like the television commercial with the group of young people gathered on a hilltop in Italy to sing *I'd Like to Buy the World a Coke*. Or the iconic Coke polar bears we see every winter. Or the classic Norman Rockwell image of Santa Claus downing a Coke, which is thought to have shaped the modern-day appearance of St. Nick himself.[2] The power of Coke's brand lies in the way it has evolved to reflect our changing times while maintaining its core message of serving up innocence, refreshment, and, ultimately, happiness.

Now let's take a closer look at some of the other emotional reactions that branders attempt to evoke through their communications style in order to solidify a place in our heads and hearts. Which of your favorite brands would you add to the descriptions below?

- **I trust them to keep their word.** Trust is probably the single most important factor in creating long-term loyalty. As consumers, we need to be absolutely certain that we can rely on our favorite brands when it comes to our work, health, and families. *Companies we can depend on: FedEx, Volvo, and Johnson & Johnson.*
- **They connect me to a community.** Brands that make us feel like part of the club connect us not only to likeminded people with shared interests but also to the company itself. All you need to do is look at social media sites like Facebook, Pinterest, and Twitter to see the power of community. *Companies that connect us: Starbucks, Harley-Davidson, and Angie's List.*

- **I love their quirkiness.** Life can be complex and challenging, so a brand that makes us chuckle while delivering the goods has staying power. *Brands that bring a smile: Southwest Airlines, Zappos, and Google (if you're not familiar with Google's chuckle-power, just check out their home page on any holiday).*

- **They make me feel like one of the cool kids.** Some brands have a way of making us feel hip. Apple knew this when they pitted cool dude "Mac" against stodgy "PC" in their series of snarky commercials. *Brands that make us feel cool even if we're not: Apple, Nasty Gal Clothing, and Trader Joe's.*

- **They make my complicated life a little easier.** In our time-challenged world, who doesn't love a company that saves us time and energy? *Brands that keep it simple: Amazon, Target, and DryBar.*

- **They make me feel special.** Whether it's an everyday celebration or a major life milestone, some brands know how to make us feel pampered. *Brands that remind us we're special: Coca-Cola, DeBeers, and Nordstrom.*

- **They're doing good things for people and the planet.** We feel good when we can support companies that we believe are helping solve the world's problems—whether through education, environmental sustainability, or relief of human suffering. *Brands that are fighting the good fight: Tom's, Prius, and Kiva.org.*

YOUR BRAND STYLE: DISCOVERING YOUR UNIQUE VOICE

As iconoclastic playwright Oscar Wilde famously said, "Be yourself, everyone else is already taken." That idea of uniqueness is equally relevant when it comes to communicating your brand. Once you've defined your brand story, the next step is refining your communication style in a way that not only is unique to you but also differentiates you from competitors so that your ideal clients can find you.

While your business brand is often communicated through organizational vehicles such as your website, product or service descriptions, and company announcements, oftentimes individuals will be charged with delivering the company's brand story. Some of the most effective communication, in fact, involves key individuals speaking on behalf of the business as a whole or in regard to some specific aspect or campaign. For example, if your company has just announced a product recall because of toxins or tampering, how would you prefer to hear the bad news? Through a corporate press release or directly from the CEO of the company?

One of the most-studied crisis management cases of all time was the 1982 Tylenol tampering incident, in which seven people in the Chicago area were killed by cyanide-laced pills. Tylenol maker Johnson & Johnson's CEO James Burke took front and center with the media throughout the entire incident and not only accepted immediate responsibility but also prompted a nationwide recall, even in areas where no tampering was suspected. Ultimately, Johnson & Johnson made sweeping improvements in non-tampering safety standards for the entire industry. It was their immediate action and public transparency that kept the disaster from sounding the death knell for the company. Conversely, in what has been viewed as one of the worst examples of crisis communications, in the aftermath of the Deepwater Horizon oil spill, BP's then-CEO Tony Hayward shamelessly said on the *Today Show*, "There is no one who wants this over more than I do. I'd like my life back."

While it's unlikely that your business will ever face anything as catastrophic as either of those incidents, it's important for the individuals who deliver your company story—both the negative and positive aspects—to learn to be influential communicators. Depending upon the type, size, and structure of your business, those individuals could include the CEO or other C-level leaders; corporate spokespeople; the business unit heads most relevant to the news at hand; or, especially in the case of small businesses, the company's owner. It's up to you to determine the style that most befits your organization, but everyone can improve their odds for delivering their message in a way that connects by learning some simple strategies.

COMPASSIONATE COMMUNICATIONS

What Johnson & Johnson CEO Burke demonstrated that BP's Hayward so obviously lacked was genuine compassion. People believed that Burke cared deeply about his company's role in the death of seven people, but no one was comforted by Hayward's self-ish statements about getting back to his own life, especially when his company was at least partially responsible for the largest oil spill in the history of the petroleum industry, as well as the loss of 11 lives.

According to research by the co-authors of the book *Words Can Change Your Brain*, our brains are shaped by the types of communications we receive, starting in early childhood. Ineffective or destructive communication can lead to long-lasting negativity whereas positive words that reinforce feelings of kindness and respect can help our brains function better.[3]

The authors—Andrew Newberg, MD (director of research at the Myrna Brind Center of Integrative Medicine at Thomas Jefferson University Hospital and Medical College) and Mark Robert Waldman (professor of communication at Loyola Marymount University)—suggest that teaching children to use positive words, or what they call "compassionate communication," can help them gain emotional self-control and may even increase attention spans. As adults, by mastering some of the basic tenets of compassionate communication, we can create more intimacy and connection with others. But before creating a connection, you've got to create a basis of trust. And that has to start before you utter a single word, because if the listener doesn't trust you, he won't believe anything you have to say.

You may have heard some Sales 101 theory about how mimicking your customers' physical stance and body movements can create rapport. If your customer places a hand on the counter, you place your hand on the counter. If she pushes her hair back off her face, you push your hair back off your face. It's the same phenomenon that happens unconsciously when someone's yawn or smile makes you do the same. It turns out that those non-verbal behaviors have a solid scientific basis in what researchers call *mirror neurons*. When we observe another person making some kind of motion, a neuron in our brain fires, making us mirror that motion. There is still speculation and study on this function, and while some scientists believe it's our brain's way of helping us learn new skills through imitation, others believe it is a primal method of connecting us to one another. Whichever theory turns out to be accurate (if not both), being aware of the powerful connection that mirroring can create, when done genuinely, can be useful in creating rapport by getting others to lower their natural defenses.

Newberg and Waldman's research offers the following advice for using non-verbal behaviors, which account for as much as 93 percent of the foundation of trust-based communication.

- **Gentle eye contact.** In order to establish trust, the listener needs to read the speaker's face for signs of deceit, anger, or disrespect. Without locking stares, which can be disconcerting, create a gentle and open connection with your eyes.

- **Kind facial expression.** A calm and smiling face makes others feel instantly relaxed. But it's difficult to fake a smile, since the muscles around the mouth and eyes tighten when we are tense. To create an authentic smile before an important conversation or presentation, imagine a pleasurable moment or picture the face of your baby, spouse, or pet. Even if you don't crack a big grin, your facial muscles will soften.

- **Keep your head level.** It's important to keep your head physically level to give you an appearance of being comfortably in control. When you tilt your head to the side, you appear more tentative and less powerful. The way you hold your chin is also an indication of how you command presence: when you jut your chin forward you can seem aggressive, and when it's tipped downward you may appear overly submissive.

- **Relaxed hand and body gestures.** Speech originated from hand gestures, and the same area of the brain controls both forms of communication, that is, verbal and non-verbal. When you use physical gestures that are natural and unforced, you help others comprehend your meaning while lowering your stress levels and also those of the listener. Learning some basic relaxation exercises can help you release tension and connect more effectively. Simply shaking out your arms and legs before an important talk can help ease tension.

Now that you've got your physical bases covered, it's time to focus on your vocal tone and rate of speech, as well as the language that you use. An important element to remember in establishing trust is that your physical and verbal cues must line up. We've all had the experience of having someone say something flattering to us but with a chilly tone that belies their words. Whether we're consciously aware of the incongruent nature of their communication, we immediately feel disconnected, if not downright suspicious. These conflicting messages, known as *neural dissonance*, can evoke feelings of doubt or apprehension in the listener, the last thing you want if you're trying to establish connection.

In order to alleviate this sense of dissonance, go back to your motives—including your *why*—for the communication, as well as your conviction that you are offering something worthwhile. Ask yourself if you've earned the right to be communicating with your subject to make sure that you're not giving out conflicting messages based on your own insecurities. Once you've got your internal messaging squared away, you can improve the quality of your communication by focusing on your vocal delivery. When you're feeling confident and relaxed, you help others relax and lower any feelings of skepticism or distrust.

Make sure your voice sounds warm and engaging by keeping your pitch in a lower register. (This can be especially challenging for women, so ladies, it's worth putting in some practice time.) Our pitch tends to go higher when we're nervous, so even a few simple breathing exercises can help you lower your tone. Speaking in a monotone also sends listeners a cue that we are nervous or scared and makes them feel the same way, so be sure to moderate your inflection by consciously adding up and down notes. Try not to pepper your speech with "um," "like," or "you know," which may lead listeners to feel that you don't know your subject matter. Pauses can actually be quite powerful and give the listener a chance to catch up with you, so don't be afraid of them. Your rate of speech also tends to speed up when you're nervous, so consciously slow it down. Not only does a slower pace help the listener follow your train of thought, it allows him or her to relax and take in what you're saying.

Another critical, although sometimes underrated, component of effective communication is brevity. We see mentions of the need for succinctness as far back as *Hamlet,* in which Polonius famously cautions Laertes to keep it short, saying, "Brevity is the soul of wit." Although not a student of neuroscience, Shakespeare was undoubtedly a student of human nature and recognized that using occasional brief sentences, as well as modulating rhythms and inflections, could hold a listener's attention better than long run-ons. According to numerous research studies, the human brain can only hold onto three or four ideas at a time, so learning to make your point concisely before moving on to the next topic is critical. If you have to speak for longer periods—as, for example, when you're giving a presentation—you can make a key point and then back it up with anecdotes, data, and details to put more meat on the bones. But be aware that making multiple points may actually diminish your overall effectiveness.

This human limitation is one reason that Abraham Lincoln's Gettysburg Address is so often cited as one of the greatest speeches in American history. Although several versions of the speech exist today and which one Lincoln delivered is still a matter of debate by historians, several points are clear. The address is only ten sentences long, it contains approximately 270 words, and it took Lincoln just over two minutes to deliver it. His focus on a key point—to uphold the values set forth by our founding fathers in the Declaration of Independence—and his rousing call-to-action—that the "government of the people, by the people and for the people shall not perish from the earth"—made it not only meaningful but memorable. It is likely that those reasons, as well as its obvious historical significance, are why this speech is still memorized today.

Although Lincoln probably intended for the stirring nature of the Gettysburg Address to evoke feelings of anxiety about the war and the future of the nation, in the business world, it can be far more fruitful to temper negative words with positive. In fact, when subjects are placed in fMRI scanners and shown words such as *death*, *illness*, *pain*, or even just *no*, chemicals including cortisol and adrenalin are released, causing a surge in stress that can impair logic and other brain functions.[4] Newberg and Waldman agree that the brain responds to negative words with far more intensity than it does to positive ones. They suggest that by using a three-to-one ratio of positive messages to negative, we will foster much greater receptivity in the listener and ultimately encourage a more successful outcome. What this means for business leaders, who must assess progress as part of effective management, is that by including a healthy dose of positivity along with criticism, your listener will be able to take in your message rather than having it shut out by the brain's natural defensiveness. While some might insist that this approach is tantamount to coddling employees, I have always found inspiration to be far more motivating than intimidation.

MINDSHARE MINUTE: YOUR ORATORY STYLE

Think about some of the most famous orators in recent history and the style of communication each represents. For example, Oprah is warm and compassionate; Martin Luther King Jr. was inspiring and fiery; Bill Clinton is personal, with down-home warmth and wit; and Jerry Seinfeld is offbeat and observational. Choose an orator with whom you can identify and whose style you'd most like to emulate.

WHY CONFIDENCE IS KING (OR QUEEN)

You can fight its unfairness all you like, but people who are extroverted, confident, or even overconfident are at a definite advantage when it comes to connecting with others. Researchers at UC–Berkeley led by Dr. Cameron Anderson found that people who demonstrate confidence tend to be more successful than their peers, even when those peers have greater talents and abilities. "Our studies found overconfidence helped people attain social status," he says. "Those who believed they were better than others, even when they weren't, were given a higher place in the social ladder, and the motivation to attain higher social status therefore triggered overconfidence."[5] So what's behind this strange cycle of overconfidence leading to success leading to confidence?

In a series of experiments conducted with college students, professors, and administrative staff at UC–Berkeley's Haas School of Business, individuals who talked and participated more actively in group tasks were considered more competent, even when they handled the assignments less well than others. Mirroring what I used to call "leadership by volume" in my corporate entertainment career, in which I often had to deal with strong egos, in general knowledge tests, participants who answered more frequently and loudly were held in highest regard, even when wrong. Others in the group rarely thought of them as overconfident but considered them "terrific" or even "beloved."[6]

In one experiment, the researchers asked MBA candidates to examine a list of historical names, events, books, and poems, identifying those that they recognized. While some of the items on the list, such as Robespierre, Wounded Knee, and *Doctor Faustus*, were real, others, such as Bonnie Prince Lorenzo, Windemere Wild, and Queen Shaddock, were invented by the researchers. Subjects who included the made-up names among those they recognized were considered to be overly confident because they assumed they were far more knowledgeable than they actually were. Yet in a follow-up survey, the same overconfident individuals were those thought to have achieved the highest social status in their research groups.

Recognizing that those who are given positions of status have more power, a greater range of options, and more access to resources, people who assume they are entitled to these benefits often display a sense of confidence, reinforcing their assumed worthiness of these entitlements. The studies led researchers to conclude that it was often the desire for social status that led to—and reinforced—overconfidence. In this case, social status is defined as others' perception of the prominence, respect, and influence that these individuals deserve. In the workplace, these people are often admired, listened to, and have more clout in swaying a group discussion or decision. This research sheds some light on why overconfident people—who are rarely seen as arrogant or selfish—are so often rewarded and even promoted over their more talented peers.

Interestingly, researchers found that many of their subjects truly believed that they were more talented, socially adept, and skilled at their jobs than the testing actually reflected. In fact, in one study, a statistically improbable 94 percent of college professors concluded that their work was above average. Perhaps it's time that they took at peek at RateMyProfessors.com for a reality check on the student perspective on their abilities.

As Professor Anderson states, "Although we may seek to choose wisely, we are often forced to rely on proxies for ability, such as individuals' confidence. In so doing, we, as a society, create incentives for those who would seek status to display more confidence than their actual ability merits."[7] While Anderson and the other study authors surmised that their research would encourage people, particularly those with hiring power, to look beyond confidence to talent, their research also points to the fact that professionals need to consciously develop their confidence or at least the appearance of being confident. As a leadership coach for high-potential executives, I routinely hear people dodge the issue, mumbling excuses about not wishing to appear arrogant. But Anderson's research subjects notwithstanding, plenty of talented people could benefit greatly by taking a page from their overconfident peers' playbooks.

I would be remiss if I didn't point out some special issues related to women and confidence. Gender bias aside, some data support the conventional wisdom that women tend to minimize their value in the workplace. Not unlike the Berkeley study, researchers from Columbia University Business School and several other universities found that overconfidence results in workplace rewards. However, their study focused specifically on how men tend to exaggerate their accomplishments more than women.

In the research study, MBA candidates were given a math test and then asked to recall their scores 15 months later. The participants were given a financial incentive to report the correct score, so it was unlikely that anyone intentionally bumped up his or her test results. Nonetheless, although male and female subjects performed similarly on the test, men inflated their scores by more than 30 percent whereas women gave themselves a 14 percent bump. The men not only beefed up their scores but were rewarded with leadership positions within the testing group based on their inaccurate perceptions of their achievements. While women also exaggerated, they were far more accurate in recalling their math test scores and thus put themselves at a disadvantage compared with their male counterparts.[8]

Next, the researchers divided the group into teams for a supposed math competition, telling participants they would receive cash prizes for correct answers. In choosing leaders for the teams, the men again exaggerated their scores—this time by 40 percent—while women amped up their numbers by 20 percent. The result was that of the 33 teams, 29 picked male leaders and only four picked female leaders. The conclusion, according to researcher Ernesto Reuben, one of the study's authors and an assistant professor at Columbia Business School, is that many companies may be choosing the most confident but not the most qualified candidates. And women are the ones who are suffering, since they are less inclined to exaggerate. "Men honestly believe they're better than they are, so it's not about getting them to tell the truth. They're already telling what they think is the truth," says Mr. Reuben.[9]

So what's a woman, an introvert, or anyone who doesn't like bragging about his or her accomplishments to do? While I'm not advocating that people start tooting their own horns ad nauseam, it's clear that lack of confidence can be a career killer. Assuming that you are already among those talented and competent professionals, here are some proven strategies to help you begin to demonstrate a higher level of confidence so you can get to the next level of your career.

- **Participate at meetings.** If necessary, prepare some data or comments ahead of time so you'll have something relevant to say. Force yourself to speak more than you normally do, even if you consider it "too much." (This is doubly important for introverts.)
- **Check the news.** When you know the latest about world news, company updates, the stock market, or sports scores, you'll be able to make small talk. Women, if you know sports, jump into the dialogue. Most people will assume you don't know a hockey puck from a soccer ball, and it's up to you to prove them wrong.

- **Head for the person standing solo.** At a networking event, after you get a cocktail—or a soda if you tend to rely on alcohol as a social lubricant—head for someone who is standing alone. Chances are he's as lost as you. Ask how long he has been involved in the organization, how he spends his time (as opposed to the utterly obnoxious "What do you do?"), or where he comes from. Get the conversational ball rolling—just remember to do your part, that is, talk.

- **Sit in the front.** I taught at California State University at Northridge for a year, helping the school develop a pilot course in entertainment business. While I used to joke that students who sat in the front got automatic As, it's no joke. Most people, and not just students, enter a conference, training session, or meeting and head straight for the back of the room. Resist the urge to hide in the back; instead, be a presence at whatever event you're attending. Ask questions, chat with your peers, and introduce yourself to the presenter. If you act like a person who deserves some attention, you'll get it.

- **Dress well.** Being carefully groomed can immediately boost your confidence. If you don't know what that means in your world, it's well worth the investment in a personal shopper or stylist. In general, dress a notch above your customers, clients, and colleagues without looking like you're headed to a funeral or job interview.

- **Join Toastmasters.** A great non-profit organization that has been around since 1924, Toastmasters supports more than 13,500 clubs in 116 countries—all dedicated to helping you speak more confidently. Check out Toastmasters.org to find a location near you.

- **Focus on contribution.** Get attention off yourself by adding value to other people's projects and priorities. Whether it's a brainstorming meeting, company gathering, or community event, doing a solid for someone else is always classy.

YOUR BRAND STRUCTURE: CREATING YOUR COMMUNICATIONS TOOLKIT

Although it may seem like a lot of work initially, having a communications program in place before you actually need it can save you a ton of headaches. Your program should include both basics, such as having media materials on hand for interviews, and complex tasks, such as having a written crisis communications protocol. While you can probably never be prepared for every contingency, you should be ready for any that you can possibly anticipate.

Every company, large or small, should have the following items in their *communications toolkit*. Whether you have an internal marketing or communications team, you're outsourcing to a vendor, or you're handling it yourself, this list will give you a running start to cover most of your needs.

CORPORATE FACT SHEET

A corporate fact sheet, sometimes called a company profile, provides basic information about your company so customers and news media can get a snapshot of the business type and composition at a glance. It may include ownership information, biographies of the leadership team and executive and advisory board members, stock trading information, history of the company, details about products and services, and size and locations of the offices. Even a small company can benefit from having a well-written fact sheet because it captures a lot of the information that prospective clients, partners, and journalists might need. Make sure to update it anytime there is a change within the organization.

PRESS RELEASE

Having a press release format that you routinely use not only gives your brand a consistent and identifiable look, but it also keeps you from having to invent the wheel every time you have a news announcement to distribute to the media. Professional-quality press releases always have a dateline (date and location from which the news is being released), a media contact (person who can be contacted to provide additional information or to schedule interviews), and a headline that sums up the content of the release in a brief, catchy topic line. Although many releases sent out today are intended more to drive online search than they are to secure traditional editorial coverage, you should still follow professional rules of journalism with every news release you send out.

COMPANY ANNOUNCEMENT

Less formal announcements not specifically intended for the media should still look just as professional as a press release. This means having a professionally designed format that includes your key brand images like your logo and tagline. For example, I provide my two-page "Gill at a Glance" background profile to all the speaker bureaus that represent me so they have all the latest facts about recent keynote engagements, client testimonials, and more.

You may also want to develop a "This Just In" or "Fast Facts" info a brief that you provide to internal customers or stakeholders that provides brief snippets and informal briefings. By branding the format with a title, as well as a logo and graphics, your constituents will come to recognize different types of announcements, as well as their relative importance. For example, "Memo from the Chairman" would probably get more immediate attention and carry more weight than "Spotlight on Our Interns," but both have their place in the organizational structure and should be consistent with your brand.

CORE MESSAGES

Like insurance, it's good to have a list of core messages on hand before you actually need them. Core messages are key strategic talking points used as internal background to describe your company, products, and services. Different from a fact sheet, core messages are a list of value statements and company beliefs that can be tailored for different needs. It's well worth taking the time to write out a dozen or so clear and succinct messages that can be used in various ways, such as for advertising and marketing materials, media interviews, employee conversations, and sales presentations, as well as in your everyday conversations about your business. Here are some points to remember when developing core messages:

1. Understand that a core message is the communication of any idea, concept, fact, value, or goal to which the company consistently adheres. For example: "Libby Gill and Company is a coaching and consulting firm that focuses on helping individuals and organizations identify, articulate, and enhance their authentic value."

2. Create a menu of succinct and easy-to-understand core messages and then layer them with two or three supporting details, such as statistics, anecdotes, or case studies.

3. Keep your core messages consistent. While you will revise your messaging as your business evolves, remember that core messages are authentic and fundamental and, as such, remain consistent even as the business changes. Make sure your written materials, including your website, press releases, slide decks, handouts, and so on, all support your core message.

4. Make defining and refining messages an ongoing habit. Make sure these messages, whether spoken or written, are clear, compelling, and have the ring of truth.

MEDIA INTERVIEW TIPS

Use these strategic tips before you put anyone in front of the media. Ideally, your key executives should have some in-depth media training before they participate in any interviews on behalf of the company. For my complete list of media interview tips, visit the Mindshare Tools section on www.LibbyGill.com.

1. **Determine the outcome before the onset.** Before you pitch, promote, or agree to any media interview, predetermine your desired outcome. Consider why you want to do this interview, as well as why you might not want to be interviewed.

2. **Set some ground rules.** Although there are some battles you will not win (and in most cases should not even pick), such as asking to review or approve the piece before it goes to print, picking the photos, limiting who else will be interviewed, or slanting the focus of the piece, there are some things you can request. You can and should find out whether the piece is on assignment or freelance, how long the interview/segment will be, when the piece will run, who will be writing or reporting, what the tone or objective of the story is, and who else will be included.

3. **Never pick up the phone and agree to an interview on the spot.** Even if it sounds straightforward and the reporter is on deadline, you can ask when the deadline is and set a time to call back—even if it's in five minutes. Get your key messages—geared to this interview—in front of you and think them through instead of answering off the cuff.

4. **Anticipate the questions.** Although you may know the basic premise of the interview, think of every question that a reporter might ask and then "find the questions to fit your answers." Practice doing Q&As with a colleague to get comfortable with the tough questions. Remember to go back to your core messages for optimal results.

5. **Take control.** When the reporter sees that you are forthcoming, that you have a quotable message, and that you are taking charge of the interview (in a positive, but not pushy way), she will relinquish much of the control to you. She wants a good story that is matched to the news source's end user—not your marketing needs—and if you provide good content that meets those needs, she will relax and let you run with it. That gives you more opportunity to get your core message across, which is always the objective.

EFFECTIVE EMAIL PROTOCOL

With so much of our discourse delivered via emails these days, it's important to have some thoughtful company rules in place so that email communication doesn't get too muddy or remote. Adapt the following to fit your needs:

1. If the subject requires more than a yes or no or one-paragraph answer and time zones allow, pick up the phone. Nothing is worse than a string of emails that dance around the topic but never really get anything done.

2. Don't use email when the person is in the next office or down the hall. Unless it has to be put in writing, remind yourself that face-to-face connection is still the most effective communication method. After all, if someone says in an email,

"Sure, happy to take that off your hands" but what he really means is, "Are you shoving your work off on me again?" you need to hear his tone of voice or see his face to pick up on that.

3. Resist the urge to succumb to slang and shorthand. Even if it is email, write real sentences, use good grammar, proof your work, and, for heaven's sake, don't use the Reply All button unless it's absolutely necessary.

4. Don't send an email and think your job is done. You still need to confirm that your message was received, understood, and acted upon. Sometimes we get lulled into a false sense that we've done some actual work when all we've done is shoot out some one-way communications. Follow up!

5. Finally, do use email to say thank you, congratulations, or job well done. And be sure to copy all the relevant parties— especially those higher up the ladder—when you're paying someone a compliment.

CAPTURE THE MINDSHARE SNAPSHOT: USING HUMOR EFFECTIVELY

One of the best ways to get your message heard and understood by others is the effective use of humor. Just check out the videos that have gone viral on YouTube and you'll see that most of them are side-splittingly funny, although occasionally in a mean-spirited way. While not all individuals or organizations are adept at using humor—and you know when you aren't—if you think you can tickle the public funny bone, it's worth a little experimentation. The following story is a great example of not only picking the right communication vehicle but also striking the right chord—literally!

CHALLENGE

During her first pregnancy, singer/songwriter and nascent entrepreneur Kerri Smith came up with an idea she readily admits is "not rocket science, but to a pregnant woman who's not sleeping, it's life-changing." Her big idea? The BellyRest maternity support pillow, essentially a pillow cut in half with a fabric crater in the middle to accommodate the pregnant woman's belly. Smith says about her pillow prototype, "I slept better immediately. The pillows stayed in place when I rolled over, and it hardly took up any real estate in bed. Plus, I found that having a pillow behind me and in front of me supported my lower back and my belly and, at the same time, reduced my hip pain."[10]

She thought her idea was so good, in fact, that she decided to manufacture the pillow and market it online through BellyRest.com and Amazon. Kerri's first business bump came when she discovered that in order to sell pillows online, she had to comply with "pillow tag laws" in numerous states. The cost of these filings amounted to nearly $6,000 in unexpected fees—an enormous amount of budget and red tape for a budding entrepreneur.

TACTICS

Having heard about crowdsourcing website Kickstarter .com, a funding platform that connects creative entrepreneurs with potential investors, Kerri decided to put her songwriting skills to work. She created a hilarious rap video called "Do Not Remove Under Penalty of Law." The video features Smith in her rap persona as KDiggy with some pregnant friends, brazenly defying the law as they ruthlessly clip tags off of pillows. Much to Smith's surprise, Kickstarter rejected her video based on what it considered its political viewpoint for raising the governmental red tape issue. Undeterred, KDiggy rapped on over to similar crowdfunding platform Indiegogo.com and raised $2,000 more than she needed for the pillow tag filings. Red tape surmounted, she recently manufactured her first round of pillows, which can be purchased on her site, with a store on Amazon.com soon to follow.

MORE

Find out what Kerri believes—in addition to her great sense of humor and an extremely creative video—helped communicate her message and launch her business. Go to www .LibbyGill.com to learn more and find out what Kerri's up to next—red tape or no red tape.

In the next chapter, we'll separate out the individuals and organizations that *claim* to do good by doing well by looking at some authentic *Contributors* who've made a difference in the lives of people around the globe.

Chapter Seven

CONTRIBUTE
If Not You, Who?

"Unless someone like you cares a whole awful lot, nothing is going to get better. It's not."

—*Dr. Seuss*

WALK INTO A PANERA CARES COMMUNITY CAFE IN CHICAGO, St. Louis, or Portland and place your order for a baked egg soufflé and a cafe latte. Or if you're feeling more in the mood for lunch, maybe you'll go for the roasted turkey panini and some freshly brewed ice tea. Your experience at one of the handful of Panera "community cafes" scattered across the United States will be nearly identical to what you'd find dining at any of the 1,591 Panera Cafes in North America. Same baked-that-day fresh bread, same homemade soups, same hand-tossed salads.[1]

But there's one critical difference. At a Panera Cares Community Cafe, you pay what you can afford—even if that's nothing. That's right: eat what you want and pay what you can. Why would a for-profit business embark on this unusual social experiment? Because, well, Panera does care. Recognizing that one in four children in the United States goes without sufficient food on a daily basis, Panera is on a mission to feed both bellies and self-esteem by offering what they call "a dignified dining experience in an uplifting environment regardless of means."

The cafe located in the Lakeview area of Chicago became the fourth non-profit cafe to join the ranks during the summer of 2012, when it made the switch from the for-profit to non-profit model under the 501(c)(3) umbrella of the Panera Cares Foundation. Everything at the Lakeside location stayed pretty much the same, except that the cash registers were replaced by donation boxes, and the staff began inviting customers to pay whatever they wanted for their coffee, soup, and sandwiches. The results have been somewhat surprising: consistent with reports from the other non-profit cafes, about 60 percent of customers voluntarily pay the suggested retail price, about 20 percent pay above retail, and the remaining 20 percent pay less or nothing at all. Revenues go into operating the stores, with any leftover cash donated to local area charities.

As Panera co-founder and co-CEO Ron Shaich describes the cafes, "They feel like every other Panera Cafe in America; they don't feel the least bit different."[2] They may not feel different, but it's a bit too early to tell whether they will make a difference to either the communities they're intended to serve or the company's bottom line. While many companies establish their own foundations or donate to non-profits, most of these organizations are only loosely associated with the day-to-day enterprise of the company. In this case, however, a for-profit store was literally transformed into a non-profit one. According to Robert Gertner of the University of Chicago's Booth School of Business, "It's very rare where you see companies where their charitable activities are a nonprofit version of what they do."[3]

Gertner points to longtime social activist company Ben & Jerry's "partner shops," for which the company waived franchise fees, allowing local non-profits to open ice cream stores. The strategy didn't work well for Ben & Jerry's, and now only three partner shops are in operation, when once there were more than a dozen. But that failure may have been more a factor of the company's often-troubled management than a problem with the concept. So far, the Chicago cafe is paying for itself, as the other community cafes have. But don't look for a massive ramp-up anytime soon. As Panera spokeswoman Kate Antonacci says, "We won't announce elaborate growth plans. We want to make sure this concept works and continues to work."[4]

THE CONSCIENTIOUS CONSUMER

If you asked a random group of people whether they were in favor of name-your-price cafes, more computers in classrooms, or advancements in wind energy, chances are most would say yes. After all, what's not to like? Don't we all want a better world for ourselves and our children?

Put that question in a different context, though, and you may get a very different answer. That is, as a consumer, are you willing to pay more for goods and services produced in an eco-friendly and humanitarian way (assuming you can define what that entails and then confirm that it has taken place)? Or, as a corporate executive or company shareholder, are you willing to sacrifice profits in the short term for what *might*—no guarantees, mind you—increase profits in the long term and *possibly* make the world a better place?

While most of us like to think we are doing our part—both personally and professionally—to serve the public interest, the idea of *service* is a complicated concept on many levels. In this chapter, we'll look at how companies contribute in socially responsible ways *and* make money at the same time—or, in other words, how they simultaneously do well and do good.

Notice I didn't say *if* they can do well and do good, but *how*. There's a rapidly growing body of evidence to support the idea that consumers want to trade with companies that are committed to helping people and the planet in tangible ways. And these consumers are willing to put their bucks where their beliefs are, even if it costs them a little more.

MARKETING TO MOMS AND MILLENNIALS

Two key market segments are driving this shift toward conscientious consumerism: moms and Millennials. According to a research study by the Boston-based AMP Agency and Cone Communications, Millennials—that is, young people born between the late 1980s and 2000—are considered one of the most civic-minded generations in history.[5] More similar to their 1930s Great Depression–era ancestors than their boomer or Gen X parents, these young people have grown up with international terrorism, global warming, and Facebook. Technology has allowed them to not only watch world events unfold but also comment on them. For many, this has resulted in a mindset of activism and compassion, occasionally tempered with a sense of caution.

Having lived through disasters such as Hurricane Katrina and 9/11, these young people have witnessed a spectrum of reactions from government and individuals ranging from the shameful lack of appropriate and timely response to Katrina's victims to the post-9/11 outpouring of love and support. And as service projects have become a routine part of the curricula of many schools and organizations, most Millennials have become accustomed to working on social and environmental projects, often in groups. Ask today's young people about the volunteer projects in which they've involved, and you're likely to hear about planting trees, tutoring kids, or working in a soup kitchen. These experiences are not only leading Millennials to a habit of lifelong service but are also influencing their buying triggers. Here are some of the findings about this generation from Cone and AMP's Millennial Cause Case Study:

- Eighty-three percent trust a company more if they are socially and environmentally responsible.
- Sixty-six percent will recommend products and services if they believe the company is socially responsible.
- Sixty-nine percent consider a company's social and environmental commitment when deciding where to shop.

- Quality and price being equal, 89 percent are willing to switch to another brand if the second brand is associated with a good cause.

Despite their youth, college-age Millennials currently have a combined $40 million in discretionary income up for grabs. And younger Millennials with similar values will soon be joining the conscientious consumer pool. This study, reinforced by research from firms including Edelman and Nielsen, provides the basis for a compelling argument: if you are courting the consumers of tomorrow, you'd better be thinking about the causes you support today.

Similar to the Millennial generation in the significance they place on cause-oriented companies are *mom consumers*, who control a whopping 80 percent of household shopping dollars. Many of these consumers have Millennial children, which can increase their commitment to buy from socially responsible companies. In fact, the desire to trade with those companies has grown 26 percent since 2008, according to Edelman's Global Purpose study.[6]

And even as new issues emerge, the causes about which moms and Millennials care remain surprisingly constant. The only perceptible shift since the recent recession has been a slight trend toward wanting companies to contribute to causes that hit closer to home. The following, in rank order of importance, are the issues closest to consumer moms' hearts:

1. Economic development, including job creation and income generation
2. Health and disease
3. Hunger
4. Education
5. Clean water access

    6. Disaster relief

    7. Environment

    8. Homelessness and housing

    9. Crime and violence prevention

    10. Equal rights and diversity

With 84 percent of moms on social media sites versus 74 percent of the general adult population, according to the Consumer Electronics Association, it's clear that moms are plugged in.[7] Critically important is the "word of mouse" aspect, which describes moms' habit of actively sharing information to help others with buying decisions. Studies show that nearly 95 percent of moms trust recommendations from people they know, and as many as 76 percent trust information posted by others online.[8]

Also worth noting: moms and Millennials are most loyal to companies that are loyal to one cause over the long term. They want to see the impact—right down to the specific actions—an organization has made to help solve a social or an environmental problem. If you are ignoring the power of these technologically savvy and uber-connected groups, you're missing the two biggest segments of decision-makers and influencers out there. And with moms and Millennials leading the charge for a better world, can others be far behind?

MINDSHARE MINUTE: THE POWER OF THE "MOMMY BLOGGERS"

With nearly 4 million "mommy bloggers" online, imagine the impact you could make if you reached just a few of these powerful influencers. They're not just talking about kids, either. These writers discuss everything from fitness to finance to technology and are said to be more influential than the *New York Times*. Check out this diverse range of mom bloggers to see what's going on in their world and how you can best relate to them: *TheBloggess .com*, *ParentsHack.com*, *DesignMom.com*, *Dooce.com*, and *TheDivineMissMommy.com*.

THE DEBATE BETWEEN DOING GOOD AND DOING WELL

It's not easy, however, to determine which companies are truly practicing what's come to be known as *corporate social responsibility* (CSR) as part of their regular business operations. Next, it's difficult to gauge the direct impact of socially positive imperatives on either the public interest or corporate profits because so many variables have to be considered. At its most basic, the *doing good* versus *doing well* debate is a balancing act between serving humankind and making money. Ultimately, you have to decide where you draw the line as both a consumer and a businessperson based on what's most important to you.

THE PROFIT IMPERATIVE

For those who are firm believers in the idea that profits come first—and there are many—the argument is simple. Companies, and particularly public companies, have an obligation to boost profits and create value for shareholders without unwarranted or irrelevant digressions. Period.

Sometimes companies get lucky and public interest aligns with corporate profit-making. Then there's really no argument. Consider

McDonald's and other quick-serve outlets' move to bring healthier eating options into their restaurants. Many companies have found that by offering fruits, salads, and whole-grain baked goods, they can expand their menus and potentially create new revenue streams, all while serving the need—and public pressure—to fight obesity and childhood diabetes. It's a win-win decision, although many would argue that bringing healthy foods into fast-food joints is purely a marketing ploy and has little to do with public health.

More often, a chasm exists between profitability and public good. And, as the argument goes, most executives are hired to maximize profits, not promote environmental sustainability; improve education; feed the hungry; or engage in any other activities that divert resources, attention, time, or manpower from the business imperative of financial growth. Presumably, if executives put those goals above building the bottom line, they should—and probably would—be replaced by managers more responsible to the business needs of the company. For private companies, of course, this is a matter of choice more than fiduciary obligation, but many of the same issues apply even when the money is coming out of your own pocket.

David Vogel is a professor at UC Berkeley's Haas School of Business and the author of *The Market for Virtue: The Potential and Limits of Corporate Social Responsibility.* In an article he wrote for *Forbes,* he effectively argues that while it is "seductive" to believe that corporate responsibility has a payoff, little hard evidence supports that notion. Vogel cites a number of companies with strong CSR performance who have done poorly financially, as well as companies with abysmal CSR track records who have done very well in terms of profitability and shareholder value.[9]

Starbucks, for example, has built a strong reputation for generous business practices and support of local farms in developing countries. And yet they have lost market share in recent years, arguably due to over-expansion. Vogel points out similar situations with CSR heavyweights Whole Foods, Timberland, and Levi Strauss—all of whom have socially responsible business practices but struggling bottom lines.

Conversely, Exxon-Mobil has an extremely negative CSR image based on their seeming indifference to playing a role in global climate change or exploring alternatives to fossil fuels. And yet they remain one of the world's most profitable corporations. Their competitor BP has, until recently, had a better CSR track record as a supporter of greenhouse gas reduction as well as an apparent willingness to explore fuel alternatives. Exxon has been more successful at avoiding and controlling spills than BP, however, which was at the helm of the Deepwater Horizon oil spill, the largest and most devastating spill in the history of the petroleum industry. Given the operational complexity of most multi-national companies, as well as varying internal standards, it can be difficult to determine:

1. Whether a company is truly practicing the tenets of corporate social responsibility
2. Whether their CSR policies have any impact on their bottom line
3. How to judge a company that may have one business unit operating responsibly but another unit within the same company ignoring socially responsible practices

The bottom line, according to Vogel—and he is far from alone in his opinion—is that while social responsibility may in itself be a worthy goal, it has no place in the corporate profit-making machine and is best addressed by others outside that realm.

DO GOOD, DO WELL, OR DO BOTH

Just who those others are, beyond the obvious non-profit organizations, is the sticking point. Until recently, many academics and experts on business ethics agreed with Vogel's assumption. Governments, they argued, with their regulatory practices and financial oversight, should be solving economic and social problems for their citizens.

But it appears that the business community is finally catching up with the conscientious consumers. The conversation began to shift at the World Economic Forum in Davos, Switzerland in 2012.[10] Almost across the board, business leaders agreed that private companies *must* be part of the solution. Following the recent recession—which some point out is still under way—attendees acknowledged that their debt-laden governments couldn't possibly solve humankind's greater financial and social ills as they struggled with seemingly endless political problems. Conversely, today's multinationals may be in a far stronger position to help than governments. Having expanded beyond borders and into competitor companies as they forge alliances with other global entities, private corporations are often more interconnected than governments—even those governments that are generally friendly and cooperative.

The takeaway from these summits? It is no longer a question of *whether* companies need to help but of *how* they will tackle these issues. There's no argument about the core challenge: profits are often at odds with the greater social good. But now experts are beginning to agree that if we don't forgo some of those profits, then we do so at our peril. While at the summit, Lynn Stout, a professor at Cornell Law School, attacked the basic premise that shareholder value has to be upheld at all costs, stating that the notion is a relatively new concept that needs to be put to rest. Stout pointed out numerous examples of corporations adding to our economic and social ills, if not causing them outright. Looking at a period of 25 years during which businesses focused primarily on creating shareholder value, Stout noted, in a perhaps unintentionally ironic understatement, "We all know it's not working out well."[11]

It wasn't just the theorists or academics who sided with Stout, but also the hardcore businesspeople. Jochen Zeitz, the chairman of PUMA and chief sustainability officer of parent company PPR, seconded the idea that it was time for corporations to step up and face global problems head on. But he also gave the group a reality check, reminding them that solving social problems and making money is unlikely to be a win-win. As Zeitz said, "Sustainability doesn't come for free." Arguing that corporate leaders should be judged on more holistic measures than mere profits, he stated, "We can't walk around saying sustainability will always be good for business. It can be good for the bottom line, but it happens in the long term. We have to think long term and balance the short-term pressures that we are under."[12]

Few people think it's going to be easy to be true global contributors, especially in a world that craves instant information, nonstop activity, and continual gratification. Here's a fairly shocking example of our increasing need for speed in economic matters: as recently as the 1960s, the average holding period for a piece of stock was eight years. Today, it's four months. The question remains: in our rapid-fire financial world, do we really have the patience to think long term? What are the costs if we don't?

ONE FOR ONE

For some companies, there is no debate between doing good and doing well. For entrepreneurs like Blake Mycoskie, doing good is non-negotiable. Mycoskie founded Los Angeles–based TOMS Shoes in 2006. It was no accident that public service was given equal, if not greater, priority than profits in this unusual company whose slogan is "One for One." The company's pitch has always been that if you buy one pair of shoes, another pair will be donated to someone in need. Millions of shoes later, TOMS is a leader in what some retail experts are calling *compassionate consumerism.*

Mycoskie's success with TOMS may be impressive, but it's just one more milestone for the entrepreneur who founded his first business while still in college. Recruited to play tennis at Southern Methodist University, he started EZ Laundry Service, with his fellow students as customers. It wasn't long until his company—which eventually supported 40 employees and eight trucks—was servicing seven colleges in the Southwest. After selling the business to his partner, coming in second on reality adventure show *The Amazing Race*, partnered with his sister; launching a reality TV cable channel; and founding a viral marketing firm, Mycoskie went on a vacation to South America that changed his life—and the lives of millions of other people, mostly children.

While visiting Argentina, Mycoskie was introduced to the *alpargata*, the traditional rope-soled shoes worn by farmers, similar to what we might call espadrilles. Enamored with the simple elegance of the shoe and at the same time appalled by the number of children and adults who had no shoes, Mycoskie decided to take action. Recognizing that the lack of shoes led to disease and infection, as well as exclusion from the education system, Mycoskie returned to Los Angeles with 250 pairs of *alpargatas* and an idea. He decided that for every pair of shoes he sold, he would donate a new pair to someone in need. After selling 10,000 pairs of shoes, he returned to Argentina with friends and family members—and 10,000 additional pairs to give to any kid who needed shoes.[13]

Now, just six years later, Mycoskie and TOMS have given away more than 2 million pairs of shoes to people in 40 countries around the world. His annual One Day Without Shoes event raises awareness about the need to help those living in poverty. In 2012, thousands of people participated in One Day Without Shoes at more than 3,000 events held in 50 countries and on more than 275 campuses around the globe. Clearly, TOMS has rallied a loyal audience of Millennials around a tangible and solvable cause that is the basis of his brand.

TOMS recently launched their second product line with TOMS Eyewear, expanding upon their successful brand and business model. When a customer buys a pair of eyeglasses, another person is helped with his or her sight challenge through the donation of prescription glasses, sight-preserving surgery, or medical treatment. With so many problems to solve in the world, why did Mycoskie—now the designated "Chief Giving Officer" of TOMS—choose to focus on eyesight?

According to the website for TOMS Eyewear, Mycoskie saw the incredible power of his simple one-buyer-to-one-donation ratio and decided that TOMS could do more than offer shoes.[14] He settled on eyesight because it is such a fundamental need, and life without sight, much like life without shoes, is incredibly difficult. Sticking with their strategy of one eye health product or service for one pair of eyeglasses purchased, TOMS is continuing to build their cause-related brand. Among the reasons TOMS took on this particular challenge are:

- It's a solvable problem. Even though eye problems are considered the seventh greatest health impairment, 80 percent of people with eyesight challenges can be helped—some with as little as a pair of prescription glasses or a 15-minute cataract operation.

- Eyesight challenges and poverty are interrelated, with 90 percent of visual impairment found in developing countries. Improve eyesight and you improve someone's chances at breaking the cycle of poverty.

- Sight and education go hand in hand. With 90 percent of children suffering from visual impairment or blindness not able to attend school, improving eyesight can open up the possibilities of education to many people who are now excluded.

- Two-thirds of the world's blind are women, mostly because in poor countries, men get preferential treatment when it comes to health care. By offering local eye care services, women and girls get a better chance at healthy sight.

- Proper glasses and medical treatment can provide immediate impact and relief. Lives can literally be transformed in a matter of days or sometimes even minutes.

CAUSE MARKETING MISFIRES

While TOMS Shoes has become a model for compassionate consumerism, with social service an integral part of not only its business model but also its brand, not all companies have been so successful with their cause-related marketing efforts. The concept of cause marketing, and even the term itself, is relatively new. The idea was born in the early 1980s when American Express joined forces with the non-profit group dedicated to restoring the Statue of Liberty.[15] Amex gave a portion of every purchase made using their cards, plus an additional amount every time a new credit card account was opened, to the restoration efforts. In addition, they sponsored a $4 million advertising campaign to encourage others to help save our national treasure. The Restoration Fund raised more than $1.7 million, the use of American Express cards rose 27 percent, and new card applications increased by 45 percent year to year. Amazingly, this all occurred in the span of a three-month campaign.

While many cause-related marketing campaigns have worked well, others have been brand backfires. One campaign that has received criticism is Skechers' BOBS Shoes, which launched in 2010. From the shoes' cushy slip-on design to the one-syllable man's name to the "buy a pair of shoes and we'll donate a pair to a child in need," BOBS has been accused of blatantly ripping off TOMS' charitable model. And while there's plenty of misery to go around and BOBS should be applauded for wanting to do their part to help, their derivative approach has raised the ire of consumers. And rightfully so, since their "me, too" style smacked of shameless marketing rather than an authentic desire to serve.

Obviously, a well-chosen cause and thoughtful execution of the surrounding initiatives can be effective tools in building brand awareness while doing some good for the world. But when the company's brand and the social cause don't align, the company can come off as manipulative and exploitative. Probably the best-known example of this kind of "what were they thinking?" cause-related marketing campaign was KFC's "Buckets for the Cure," which was linked to breast cancer awareness. KFC went so far as to change the color of the fried chicken buckets from red to pink, only to be widely ridiculed, along with its sponsoring partner, Susan G. Komen for the Cure.[16]

Apparently, no one thought about the fact that deep-fried chicken has been directly linked to obesity, which increases the risk of breast cancer. The Center for Media and Democracy's website *PR Watch* dubbed this kind of campaign "pink washing," or using pink ribbon–designated goods to promote breast cancer awareness while selling products that are linked to disease or injury.[17] The remedy, of course, is to deeply consider the cause's authenticity and relevance to your business before creating an entire campaign around it. If you want to maintain your brand integrity, it's better to do nothing at all than to implement an ill-conceived campaign better left in the conference room.

ROCK STARS OF THE NEW ECONOMY

As tricky as it can be to recognize companies that genuinely contribute to the social good, one organization has made it its mission to identify and advocate for "triple bottom line" companies—that is, those corporations that measure performance in terms of people and the planet, as well as profits. B Lab, a non-profit that certifies socially responsible corporations with their "B Corps" designation, was founded by entrepreneur Jay Coen Gilbert and private equity investor Andrew Kassoy. Both are fellows at the Aspen Institute, an educational and policy studies organization headquartered in Washington, DC, with a campus in Aspen, Colorado. B Lab started life as Gilbert's values-based leadership project for the institute, with Kassoy joining him in the effort.[18]

The initial idea of the *benefit corporation* (*B corp*) was conceived in early America to help create companies that aided the public by building roads, bridges, and other public works and is now being revived by socially conscious organizations to meet our current social and environmental needs. B Lab (the B stands for benefit and/or "B the change you want to see in the world") says its B Corps certification is to sustainable business what fair trade certification is to coffee or USDA organic certification is to milk. "We're LEED for business," says Gilbert, referring to the rigorous Leadership in Energy and Environmental Design certification process for design and construction ventures.[19] To be certified by B Lab, B Corps must meet similarly stringent standards, but with a focus on social and environmental performance, accountability, and transparency. In order to drive lasting change, prove that their intentions are more than a passing management whim or a superficial gesture, and qualify for the certification, companies are required to write specific and detailed social responsibility policies into their charters and bylaws.

As Gilbert recently told attendees at a TED talk in Philadelphia, lacking supportive corporate laws and proper standards makes it difficult for a socially responsible business to scale "with the speed commensurate with the need."[20] But by using what they call "the power of business" to solve social and environmental issues, B Lab is attempting to make those changes possible by concentrating on three interconnected initiatives:

1. Building a community of certified B Corporations so that consumers and investors can identify companies that are true contributors and not just great marketers.
2. Encouraging investment to directly impact these socially responsible corporations, using B Lab's Global Impact and Investment Rating System (GIIRS) Ratings and Analytics Platform.
3. Promoting legislation to create legal and corporate standards for B Corporations.

So why would a company willingly subject itself to this kind of third-party scrutiny? Basically, to gain skills and guidance in the triple bottom line best practices needed to beef up profits while doing good for the world. Or, as the B Lab website proclaims, "So many reasons. What's yours?" Some of the do-good-*and*-do-well scenarios they see among their members include companies that:

- **Lead a movement.** B Lab states that certified B Corporations are redefining success in business by translating ideas into action. Or, as *Esquire* magazine suggested, B Corps might turn out to be like civil rights for blacks or voting rights for women—eccentric, unpopular ideas that took hold and changed the world.[21]

- **Differentiate from pretenders.** With its demanding standards and objective analytics, B Lab certification offers the proof of social responsibility that investors and consumers want to see. More than marketing sleight of hand, these certifications offer measurable results.

- **Generate press.** The association with B Lab, as well as other B Corps–certified companies, gives organizations brand equity and a great story to tell. And B Lab has helped its certified organizations reach nearly 20 million people through its press coverage.

- **Benchmark performance.** By using the many tools that B Lab offers its certified organizations, companies can stay competitive and profitable—all while maintaining socially responsible standards.

- **Attract and engage top talent.** Millennials are now roughly 50 percent of our workforce. As we've seen, they have a deep personal commitment to social causes. In fact, according to Cone and AMP's research on Millennials, 61 percent of 13- to 25-year-olds say they feel personally responsible for making a difference in the world, and an encouraging 81 percent report having volunteered within the past year.[22] In a Deloitte survey of 18- to 26-year-olds, 61 percent of participants said they would like to work for a company that offers volunteer opportunities.[23] These dedicated young people are not only changing the way we think, they're changing the way we work.

- **Demonstrate deep commitment.** B Corps certification confirms a company's commitment to its workforce as well as its community. Check out the great job board at www.bcorporation .net/community/b-corp-jobs for current postings with purpose.

As B Lab's Gilbert says, "Government and non-profits are necessary but insufficient"[24] to solve the enormous problems our society is facing. But B Lab is poised to meet the challenge. So far B Lab has certified more than 650 corporations in 19 countries and 60 industries. B Lab calls the latest of these certified organizations the "Rock Stars of the New Economy" with good reason. Here are just a few of those innovative superstars who have built brands that inspire conscientious consumers with their drive to solve problems, even as they're making profits.

FREELANCE INSURANCE COMPANY

Sara Horowitz is the founder and executive director of the non-profit Freelancers Union and CEO of the for-profit social purpose–driven Freelancers Insurance Company. A MacArthur Foundation Genius Fellow, Horowitz is a long-time leader in social responsibility and a champion for independent workers. Freelancers now make up 30 percent of our country's workforce but have historically been at a disadvantage when it comes to the protection, benefits, and support that traditional employees receive in the workplace. Horowitz founded the Freelancers Union—which now has more than 170,000 members nationwide—to establish a new type of union to serve today's workers while helping to solve social problems.

Recognizing the need for independent workers to benefit from reliable, affordable health insurance, Horowitz went on to found the Freelancers Insurance Company (FIC) in 2009, providing coverage that could easily travel with freelancers from job to job. Based on the idea that independent employees in a community are "stronger and safer than on our own," FIC members can obtain lower-cost health insurance and minimize risks as a group more effectively than they could as individuals. FIC is a B Corps company that puts sustainability above getting rich, funneling all of its profits back into the organization so it can continue to provide high-quality health care to its members. As the FIC website states, "Feedback from our members drives our continuous evolution, and we hope that our efforts will begin to change the way Americans think about, consume, and pay for health care in the years to come."[25]

SUNGEVITY

As part of what it calls the "rooftop revolution," Sungevity wants to bring solar power to the masses, and they do it by more than just installing panels on your roof. Sungevity will handle all the paperwork and permitting and, in some cases, lease solar panels to you with no down payment. Plus, the Sungevity solar home care team troubleshoots the installation and maintenance.

A B Corps company, Sungevity was founded by clean-tech entrepreneur Danny Kennedy. A passionate environmental activist, Danny was formerly the campaign manager for Greenpeace Australia Pacific. He also ran Greenpeace's California Clean Energy Campaign, which helped produce the current California Solar Initiative, a program that offers individuals cash back for installing solar technology in their home or business. Sungevity emphasizes fiscal responsibility along with energy independence. Since having their solar panels installed, many of their customers report zero maintenance problems and zero energy bills. How's that for energy efficiency?[26]

BETTER WORLD BOOKS

As a lover of books, it really upset me to learn that every year more than one billion books end up in landfills—especially when books are such rare and precious commodities in many parts of the world. Fortunately, it upset two students from the University of Notre Dame in South Bend, Indiana, so much that they decided to do something about it. They created Better World Books, a B Corps triple bottom line business that collects and sells unwanted "orphan" books and uses the proceeds to fund 80 non-profit literacy partner organizations, including Books for Africa, Worldfund, the National Center for Family Literacy, and Room to Read.[27]

What started as a simple quest to sell their old textbooks online turned into a mission for classmates Christopher "Kreece" Fuchs and Xavier Helgesen. After Fuchs quickly sold their books for a better price than they would have gotten from the campus bookstore, Helgesen smelled a potential entrepreneurial venture and went looking for more books. The guys were shocked to discover that in an attempt to make room for new titles, bookstores, colleges, and even libraries dumped millions of books every year.

The pair drafted former classmate and investment banker Jeff Kurtzman, and they decided to create a company that, in addition to selling books, would fund literacy causes worldwide, giving people a chance and a means to succeed. As they envisioned it, the business wouldn't just have a sideline social benefit—the social benefit would be its *raison d'être*. They wrote a business plan for the company, entered it into a contest at Notre Dame, and won the

"Best Social Venture" category and $7,000 in prize money to get them started.

Unable to compete with bookselling giants like Amazon.com or Barnes & Noble, Better World Books relies on the emotional connection it makes with its customers. When you purchase a book, you receive an email ostensibly from the book you've just bought, complimenting you on your literary taste, thanking you for getting it off the shelf where it has been languishing next to "drama queen" neighbor *Jane Eyre*, and saving it from becoming part of a landfill. To people who love books and want to share them with the world, this note makes your purchase all the more personal.

So far, these literary superheroes have saved 8,000 tons of books from landfills. *That's more than 16.5 million books!* In addition to their efforts to protect the environment by limiting their carbon footprint, they are also committed to their "Book for Book" program, in which they donate one book for every book purchased. And as the running count on their website banner proudly proclaims, as of the writing of this book, they have donated 6,742,292 books, raised $13,145,860.49 in funds for literacy organizations and libraries, and reused or recycled 95,152,590 books. They certainly appear to be living up to their goal of changing the world—one book at a time.

BRAND BUILDING BLOCK #6: B THE CHANGE

As you can see from these profiles on companies that *Contribute* like Panera, Better World Books, TOMS Shoes, Sungevity, and the Freelance Insurance Company, lots of folks are dedicated to taking care of people and the planet, all while turning a profit. But even if you make no claim to being a triple bottom line business, you can still make a difference in your community, get your workforce engaged, and give your brand a boost all at the same time.

According to studies, 80 percent of Americans prefer to do business with companies that support social causes, while 72 percent of employees say they'd like their employers to do more in support of these issues.[28] So what can you, as an individual or as part of an organization, do to make a contribution? Check out the following strategies to see how you can support causes in your own neighborhood, across the globe, or both.

- **Choose a charity or cause that fits your brand.** You need to carefully consider your core business as well as your products and services before strategically choosing a charity or cause that authentically fits your brand and makes sense to your customers. Target and the Target Foundation give millions of dollars to causes in the communities where they are located. Since 1946, they've given 5 percent of their profits to support education, social services, and the arts right in the neighborhoods where their customers live and shop. Kroger, the supermarket chain, supports food banks through a hunger-fighting charity called Feeding America. *Good causes, good brand sense.*

- **Determine how you can further the cause.** Find ways to get personally involved in your cause by either supporting the charitable organization itself or directly helping the population that it serves. You might donate goods or services, get your colleagues or employees involved in activities, serve as an advisor or a board member, or sponsor a campaign or an event. Tide's Loads of Hope brings its giant mobile laundromat to areas devastated by natural disasters, and their volunteers wash, fluff, and fold the clothes of those afflicted, all for free.[29] *Discover how best you can serve, craft a plan, and dive in.*

- **Measure your results.** If there are no metrics or measurements for effectiveness, you'll never know whether you're spending your time, energy, and hard-earned money on a cause that works. And neither will your customers and clients. Do your homework using online research sites like CharityNavigator.com, which evaluates non-profits based on financial health, accountability, and transparency. *Ask tough questions and expect answers.*

- **Communicate your cause to your customer base.** Although it used to be considered slightly tacky, if not unethical, to toot your own horn about charitable efforts, the thinking on that has evolved. Not only do companies want the halo effect from doing good—as well they should—but by raising awareness about their charitable efforts, they can influence others to give. Let your customers, clients, and colleagues know why you've chosen your cause, how you plan to support it, and what they can do to help—the more specific, the better. Rock School Scholarship Fund (rockschoolfund.org) "helps kids rock" by giving music scholarships to schools across the country that teach kids to sing or play rock music.[30] Executive Director Wendy Winks asks contributors for specific donation amounts—$100 buys a new instrument; $200 buys an instrument and a month of lessons; and $800 buys an instrument, four months of lessons, and the chance to perform in a live show. *Make it easy for people to understand how their contributions are actually being used.*

- **Keep up the good works.** Maintain the momentum by measuring campaign effectiveness based on your predetermined metrics. Let your audience know what's happening on a regular basis. You'll not only keep donors and potential donors engaged, but you'll be seen as someone who provides consistent, ongoing value and not a cause-marketing flash in the pan. *Don't be a fair-weather philanthropist.*

CAPTURE THE MINDSHARE SNAPSHOT: BUILDING SUSTAINABLE BUSINESSES

Building a business is difficult enough. As we've seen in this chapter, building a triple bottom line business based on ethical practices and social responsibility creates multiple layers of complexity. But that didn't stop the intrepid Carrie Norton from launching her own business—in the midst of a recession—so she could help other entrepreneurs build sustainable and environmentally conscious companies. As Norton says, "If we can transform business, we can transform the world. That's the fundamental thesis upon which I've been operating."[31]

CHALLENGE

A 2010 Catto Fellow of the Aspen Institute and co-founder of the Sustainable Business Council of Los Angeles, Norton is a passionate blend of business expertise and social consciousness. With a background in the solar energy industry and sustainable business, Norton has worked at companies including innovation incubator Idealab and Garage Technology Ventures, founded by business guru Guy Kawasaki. As Norton states, "My work at the intersection of innovation and business makes me keenly aware of what's missing out there for entrepreneurs with great ideas for solving environmental and social problems through business."

To ensure that she could make a business case for sustainability that would benefit others, Carrie spent years working in what she calls the "entrepreneurial ecosphere," an area that includes venture capital, start-ups, and early adopter clients like Google and Toyota. Through her perspective from all sides of the table, Carrie saw firsthand the many frustrations and challenges of getting ambitious projects off the ground, especially while attempting to make a profit. "It never made sense to me that philanthropy or corporate social responsibility was decoupled from the act of doing business," she said. "So I've been looking at how we can embed sustainability or triple bottom line principles into the DNA of companies from the outset."

TACTICS

Her solution? The Green Business BASE CAMP, the first dedicated high-impact immersive training program for entrepreneurs and corporate intra-preneurs, that is, executives within corporations. Carrie's goal is to help these leaders learn about sustainability as an opportunity for top-line growth, innovation, and transformative business.

She created the accelerated learning curriculum based on a foundation of *design thinking* and *biomimicry*—that is, using systems, models, and processes found in nature to solve human problems.

The intensive experiential workshop hosts participants from around the world, providing each entrepreneur with small-group learning and big-picture thinking. Students receive one-on-one coaching and mentoring, networking opportunities with likeminded peers, and the chance to pitch their businesses in front of a panel of expert judges in preparation for the real thing.

"I believe we're living in a world where everyone has to have an entrepreneurial mindset, regardless of whether or not you plan to start your own company. You have to be entrepreneurial about your educational path. You have to be entrepreneurial about your life path. And you have to be entrepreneurial about your career because the answers that were delivered to you on a silver platter in the past don't hold up anymore," she remarks. Grateful for the enthusiasm that her students bring to the training experience, Carrie admits that she sometimes wishes her "passion-preneurs" had a little more *preneur* and a little less *passion* when it comes to business, which was exactly her impetus for founding BASE CAMP.

Norton believes that we must reinvent our country and that businesspeople are best equipped for the job, but they need help to get to market quickly. "I've had the privilege of sitting around so many sides of the table, I understand the delicate dance that one does with investors to tell them the story they want to hear to get the money you need," she confides. "Look at the statistics of entrepreneurship, with failure rates so astronomically high. I fervently believe that it doesn't have to be that way."

And it won't be if she has her say. With the success of her inaugural training program, Norton is taking her mission global, with workshops planned for the United Kingdom, Brazil, Singapore, and India. As she sums it up, "Helping you bring your green business idea to market means we all win."

MORE

For more strategies on how to implement the Seven Mindshare Methods—*Clarify, Commit, Collaborate, Connect, Compete, Communicate,* and *Contribute*—in your work, visit www.LibbyGill.com to find numerous brand- and business-building tools.

Finally, let's look at the *"Eighth C"* to see how one small effort created a brand that made a big change in the lives of others.

SUMMATION
The Eighth C

Success is not final, failure is not fatal; it is the courage to continue that counts.

—Winston Churchill

NOW THAT WE HAVE NAVIGATED THE SEVEN CS—CLARIFY, COMMIT, *Collaborate, Connect, Compete, Communicate,* and *Contribute*— it's time to add one more C to the mix. And that's *Courage,* because building a successful personal or professional brand is not for the faint of heart. As you've seen throughout this book, it takes purpose and persistence to create a career, product, service, or cause that truly matters. But if you care deeply, chances are that others will too. And that's where your authentic value can make a huge difference in someone's life—or lots of someone's lives.

Although perhaps the final C should stand for *Cabbage* in honor of a little girl, a big idea, and a 40-pound cruciferous vegetable. Katie Stagliano was nine years old when she brought a cabbage seedling home from a third-grade extracurricular program. At the time, Katie recalls, she didn't expect the assignment to be a turning point in her life, just a fun thing to do. She planted, watered, fertilized, and nurtured her plant, even enlisting her grandfather to help her build a protective fence—or "cabbage cage"—around it when deer were spotted grazing in the area. Katie's cabbage grew to an astounding 40 pounds, almost as big as she was at the time.[1]

Knowing she had something very special on her hands, Katie thought about what she should do with the cabbage. "My dad said not to take anything for granted, and that there were lots of people without any food who had to go to soup kitchens," she remembers. Katie barely knew what a soup kitchen was, let alone that there were any in her town. But after she and her mom contacted several facilities, they found one that was thrilled to accept the donation of Katie's cabbage. To the little girl's amazement, that one cabbage fed more than 275 people in the form of cabbage soup. She saw firsthand how many people relied on soup kitchens for what might be their only hot meal of the day, if not their only meal. Realizing how many people she could help with her homegrown donations, Katie planted more gardens and began donating her harvests—dubbed Katie's Krops—to people in need.

Although Katie didn't set out to create a brand, she most certainly did. In fact, I can't think of any organization or individual who embodies the principles of capturing the mindshare better than Katie. Here are her thoughts about the seven core concepts outlined in this book:

- *Clarify*—Have a clear mission to get you started and then branch off into other related areas.
- *Commit*—When people start something, they don't always realize they are making a big commitment that will eat up hours of their time. But if your cause is important, it's worth it to keep going.
- *Collaborate*—You can't get as much done if you don't rely on other great people to help you create an amazing result. Don't try to do everything alone.
- *Connect*—When you connect with others in need, you get an entirely new perspective on the world. As Katie says, "I knew hunger was an issue, but I didn't connect it to people." Until she got her hands dirty, that is.
- *Communicate*—Katie's too focused on the work to spend much time communicating her story. But as others have discovered her, they are spreading the word. That's the beauty of having brand evangelists who want to share your story.

- *Compete*—Not surprisingly, Katie doesn't worry too much about competition. She stays focused on the mission.
- *Contribute*—Katie admits plenty of people doubted that she could make a difference in the world, especially at her age. Her advice? Stick with what you care about for the long run and never give up.

Today, Katie is fourteen, oversees more than 50 gardens, and has donated thousands of pounds of fresh produce to help feed the hungry. Katie has inspired hundreds of kids across the country to apply for grants so they can start gardens of their own, which are springing up in backyards and on rooftops, in vacant lots and behind libraries. Katie has even been honored with a Clinton Global Citizen Award for visionary leadership. Her cause—and her courage—are still growing strong. And if that's what one little girl working in a garden can do, imagine what you can do to make a difference with your brand.

KEY CHAPTER TAKEAWAYS

INTRODUCTION

The Seven Core Mindshare Methods:
Clarify, Commit, Collaborate, Connect, Compete, Communicate, and *Contribute*

CHAPTER ONE   CLARIFY: DISCOVERING YOUR EMOTIONAL ASSIGNMENT

- Do I Really Need a Brand?
- Purpose, Premise, and Promise
- Mindshare Minute: Developing Your Purpose, Premise, and Promise
- Brand Building Block #1: Names that Support Your Brand
- Vice President of First Impressions
- Join the Club
- Discovering Your Emotional Assignment
- Capture the Mindshare Snapshot: Naming of an Icon
  - Naming of an Icon
  - Challenge
  - Tactics
  - More

CHAPTER TWO   COMMIT: THE NON-NEGOTIABLE PROMISE OF EXCELLENCE

- The Pearson Archetypal System
- Kenexa and the Hero Culture
- Mindshare Minute: Excellence at Work
- The Experience of Total Excellence
- Sensory Branding
- Multi-Sensory Makes Good Sense
  - Sight Wonderful
  - Tasteful Branding
  - Brand Scents
  - See Me, Feel Me, Touch Me
- Mindshare Minute: Branded Business Card
  - Sound Decisions
- Capture the Mindshare Snapshot: The MoniMeter
  - Challenge
  - Tactics
  - More

CHAPTER THREE   COLLABORATE: CREATING YOUR BRAND ONE CONVERSATION AT A TIME

- Cooperation on Steroids
- Brand Building Block #2: Ten Techniques for Creating a More Collaborative Culture
- Managing Conflict with Communication
  - The You-I-We Approach
  - Third Good Option
  - The Four Ds
- The Brand Experience
- Environments That Elicit Collaboration
  - How Does Your Space Stack Up?
- The Confident Collaborateur
  - Identifying Your Credibility Boosters
- Creators Project

- Capture the Mindshare Snapshot: Continuing the Collaboration
  - Challenge
  - Tactics
  - More

CHAPTER FOUR   CONNECT: CREATING THE AUTHENTIC EMOTIONAL LINK

- Processing Emotions
  - Deep Limbic System
  - Prefrontal Cortex
  - Amygdala
- Connecting with Our Why
- Mindshare Minute: Crafting Your *Why* Message
- Born to Work Here
- Right from the Start
- Mindshare Minute: Building a Branded Introduction Package
- Connecting with Your Inner Entrepreneur
- The Magic of Miraval
- Brand Building Block #3: Creating the Online Connection
  - Lack of Clarity on Your Home Page
  - Confusing Site Navigation
  - Amateurish Design
  - Lousy Content
  - Not Establishing Your Credibility Upfront
  - Two Few Ways to Connect
- Capture the Mindshare Snapshot: Become a More Charismatic Connector
  - Challenge
  - Tactics
  - More

CHAPTER FIVE   COMPETE: WHAT MAKES YOU SO SPECIAL?

- Relevance as Competitive Edge
- The Many Faces of Competition

- Mindshare Minute: Identify the Competition
- Out-Collaborating the Competition
- Go Bold or Go Home
- Brand Building Block #4: Developing Your Online Brand
  - This Bud's For You: Company Slogans
- Mindshare Minute: Creating Your Sticky Tagline
- Connections That Beat the Competition
- Monitor the Competition While You Manage Your Brand
  - You Say You Want an Evolution
  - Reputation Matters
- Capture the Mindshare Snapshot: Communicating Your Competitive Edge
  - Challenge
  - Tactics
  - More

CHAPTER SIX   COMMUNICATE: "TALKING YOUR WALK" TO INFLUENCE AND INSPIRE

- We Give You a World to Work With
- Brand Building Block #5: Creating Your Brand's Story, Style, and Structure
- Your Brand Story: Once More with Feeling
- Your Brand Style: Discovering Your Unique Voice
- Compassionate Communications
- Mindshare Minute: Your Oratory Style
- Why Confidence Is King (or Queen)
- Your Brand Structure: Creating Your Communications Toolkit
  - Corporate Fact Sheet
  - Press Release
  - Company Announcement
  - Core Messages
- Media Interview Tips
- Effective Email Protocol

- Capture the Mindshare Snapshot: Using Humor Effectively
  - Challenge
  - Tactics
  - More

CHAPTER SEVEN   CONTRIBUTE: IF NOT YOU, WHO?

- The Conscientious Consumer
- Marketing to Moms and Millenials
- Mindshare Minute: The Power of the "Mommy Bloggers"
- The Debate between Doing Good and Doing Well
  - The Profit Imperative
  - Do Good, Do Well, or Do Both
- One for One
- Cause Marketing Misfires
- Rock Stars of the New Economy
  - Freelance Insurance Company
  - Sungevity
  - Better World Books
- Brand Building Block #6: B the Change
- Capture the Mindshare Snapshot: Building Sustainable Businesses
  - Challenge
  - Tactics
  - More

SUMMATION: THE EIGHTH C

NOTES

CHAPTER 1: CLARIFY

1. Brian Bowman, founder and CEO, LikeIt.com, interview with the author, July 9, 2012. (Likeit.com closed its doors in April 2013.)
2. Martin Lindstrom, author of *Buyology: Truth and Lies About Why We Buy*.
3. Seth Godin, author of *Tribes*.
4. Erica Swallow, *Forbes*, August 29, 2012.
5. Marc Hershon, interview with the author, July 17, 2012.

CHAPTER 2: COMMIT

1. Kenexa, "To Us, Business Is Personal" (video clip), http://www.kenexa .com/AboutKenexa/OurPromisetoYou.
2. Carol Pearson, "Pearson Archetypal System," http://www.herowithin .com/.
3. Libby, Gill, *You Unstuck: Mastering the New Rules of Risk-Taking in Work and Life* (Palo Alto, CA: Solas House, 2009).
4. Tim Geisert, interview with the author, August 3, 2012.
5. http://www.herowithin.com.
6. Stephanie Clifford, "Malls' New Pitch: Come for the Experience," *New York Times*, July 17, 2012.
7. Ibid.
8. Ibid.
9. ScentAir, "Why Scent," http://www.scentair.com/why-scent/.

10. Trader Joe's, "FAQs," http://www.traderjoes.com/about/general-faq .asp.

11. Jelly Belly, "Jelly Belly Factory Tours," http://www.jellybelly.com /visit_jelly_belly/california_factory_tours.aspx.

12. Maggie Koerth-Baker, "The Surprising Impact of Taste and Smell," *Live Science*, August 5, 2008, http://www.livescience.com/2737 -surprising-impact-taste-smell.html.

13. Research and Markets, www.ResearchandMarkets.com.

14. First Flavor, http://firstflavor.com.

15. CCD Innovation and Packaged Facts, "Hot and Spicy Flavors Flare Across Culinary Landscape," *Marketwire*, May 29, 2012, http://www .marketwire.com/press-release/hot-and-spicy-flavors-flare-across -culinary-landscape-1662683.htm.

16. William Grimes, "Looks Like a Taco, Tastes Like a Chip," *New York Times*, June 19, 2012.

17. AirEssentials, http://autoguide.com/auto-news/2012/04/rolls-royce -ghost-six-senses-concept-even-smells-expensive.html.

18. Nauman Farooq, "Rolls Royce Ghost 'Six Senses' Concept Even Smells Expensive," *Auto Guide*, April 23, 2012, http://www.autoguide .com/auto-news/2012/04/rolls-royce-ghost-six-senses-concept-even -smells-expensive.html.

19. Air Esscentials, "Case Studies," http://www.airesscentials.com/?q =case-studies.

20. Mindy Fetterman and Jayne O'Donnell, "Just Browsing at the Mall? That's What You Think," *USA Today*, September 1, 2006.

21. The Broadmoor–Colorado Springs, "Something in the Air...," March 20, 2012, http://www.thebroadmoorblog.com/tag/optimism/.

22. John Bargh, Christopher Nocera, and Joshua Ackerman, "Tactile Sensations Influence Social Judgments and Decisions," *Science Daily*, June 25, 2010, http://www.sciencedaily.com/releases/2010/06 /100624140908.htm.

23. Monica Nelson, "MoniMeals," http://monimeals.com/.

CHAPTER 3: COLLABORATE

1. Catherine Zoharko and Beth Volkerding, interview with the author, August 2012.

2. Jennifer Schlimgen, architect, Kahler Slater, interview with the author, August 15, 2012.

3. Walter Isaacson, *Steve Jobs* (New York: Simon and Schuster, 2011).

4. Randy Nelson, "Learning and Working in the Collaborative Age" [video], *Edutopia*, September 10, 2008, http://www.edutopia.org /randy-nelson-school-to-career-video.

5. Patti Cotton, professional mediator, interview with the author, August 1, 2012.

6. Kahler Slater, http://www.kahlerslater.com/.

7. Schlimgen, interview.

8. Ibid.

9. Ibid.

10. Kahler Slater, "What Makes a Great Workplace?" http://www .kahlerslater.com/content/pdf/What-Makes-a-Great-Workplace -white-paper.pdf.

11. Schlimgen, interview.

12. Kahler Slater white paper, "What Makes a Great Workplace?"

13. Bee Shyuan-Chang, "In the Midnight Hour, A Second Wind," *New York Times*, October 11, 2011.

14. Eliot Van Buskirk, "Intel and Vice Launch Creators Project: Selling Out or Boosting Creativity?" *Wired*, May 10, 2010.

15. Andrew Katz, "You're Fired … Wait You're Hired … Again," *Welcome to the World of HR*, http://astronsolutionsworldofhr.blogspot.com /2010/08/youre-firedwaityoure-hiredagain.html.

CHAPTER 4: CONNECT

1. Adam Tschorn, "Marilyn Monroe Nail Salons, Cafe in the Works," *Los Angeles Times*, July 29, 2012.

2. Simon Sinek, *Start With Why: How Great Leaders Inspire Everyone to Take Action* (New York: Portfolio Trade, 2011).

3. Tamara Monosoff, interview with the author, October 13, 2012.

4. Charles Baldwin, chief administrative officer, Cabela's, interview with the author, September 10, 2012.

5. http://www.cabelas.jobs/culture.html.

6. "The Culture of Cabela's: Internal Study Leads to Higher Employee Engagement and Productivity," white paper.

7. Reid Hoffman and Ben Casnocha, *The Startup of You: Adapt to the Future, Invest in Yourself, and Transform Your Career* (New York: Crown Business, 2012).

8. Michael Tompkins, Miraval CEO, interview with the author, July 27, 2012.

9. Margie Aliprandi, entrepreneur, interview with the author, November 26, 2012.

CHAPTER 5: COMPETE

1. Alexandra Bruell, "How Zumba Built a Brand with a Cult Following in Just a Few Years," *Advertising Age*, August 20, 2012.

2. Alexandra Bruell, Adage.com, August 20, 2012.

3. Kevin Gray, Reuters, June 24, 2012.

4. Ibid.

5. Ibid.

6. Issie Lapowsky, "Zumba Turns Dancers Into Entrepreneurs," *Inc. Mag*, May 26 2012, http://www.inc.com/articles/2010/05/zumba-fitness-entrepreneurs.html.

7. David Aaker, *Brand Relevance: Making Competition Irrelevant* (San Francisco: Jossey-Bass, 2011).

8. Bianca Ramirez and Susanne Whatley, "Trevor Denman Starts His 30th Season as the Voice of Santa Anita Park Horse Racing," *Southern California Public Radio*, October 31, 2012, http://www.scpr.org/news/2012/10/31/34800/trever-denman-his-30th-season-voice-santa-anita-pa/.

9. Ibid.

10. John Sullivan, senior director of strategies and effectiveness, Kao USA, interview with the author, August 2, 2012.

11. Karen Frank, vice president of marketing, Kao USA, interview with the author, August 2, 2012.

12. Ivan Arreguin-Toft, *How the Weak Win Wars: A Theory of Asymmetric Conflict* (New York: Cambridge University Press, 2006).

13. Sullivan, interview.

14. Victoria Barret, "Nasty Gal's Sophia Amoruso: Fashion's New Phenom," *Forbes*, June 2012.

15. Flash Steinbeiser, "Fashion Start-up Nasty Gal Raises $40M," *Inc.com*, August 27, 2012.

16. Andrea Chang, "Nasty Gal Clothing—As Red Hot As Its Founder's Lipstick," *Los Angeles Times*, August 26, 2012.

17. Harry S. Dent Jr. and Rodney Johnson, "Why Harley Won't Regain Its Highs of 2006," *Survive and Prosper's Instablog*, May 30, 2012, http://seekingalpha.com/instablog/3177621-survive-prosper/680781-why-harley-wont-regain-its-highs-of-2006.

18. Harley Davidson, "Garage Party," http://www.harley-davidson.com/en_US/Content/Pages/women-riders/garage-party.html.

19. http://www.harley-davidson.com/en_US/Content/Pages/learn-to-ride/boot-camp.html#mbcvideos/1.

20. Jesse McKinley, "Born to Be Wild, Aging Bikers Settle for Comfy," *New York Times*, September 13, 2012.

21. Harris Interactive, February 13, 2012, http://www.harrisinteractive.com/Home.aspx.

22. Ibid.

23. John Sullivan, senior director of strategies and effectiveness, Kao USA, interview with the author, August 2, 2012.

CHAPTER 6: COMMUNICATE

1. Heather Rim, vice president, Global Corporate Communications Group, Avery Dennison, interview with the author, August 16, 2012.

2. Coca-Cola Conversations staff, "The True History of the Modern Day Santa Claus," January 1, 2012, http://www.coca-colacompany.com/stories/coke-lore-santa-claus.

3. Andrew Newberg and Mark Robert Waldman, *Words Can Change Your Brain: 12 Conversation Strategies to Build Trust, Resolve Conflict and Increase Intimacy* (New York: Hudson Street Press, 2012).

4. http://scan.oxfordjournals.org/content/early/2012/05/17/scan.nss034.abstract.

5. http://www.haas.berkeley.edu/news/20120813anderson.html.

6. Cameron Anderson, Sebastien Brion, Don A. Moore, and Jessica A. Kennedy, "A Status-Enhancement Account of Overconfidence," *Journal of Personality and Social Psychology* (forthcoming), haas.berkeley.edu/faculty/papers/anderson/status%20enhancement%20account%20of%20overconfidence.pdf.

7. Ibid.

8. Leslie Kwoh, "Tall Tales: Do Men Exaggerate More?" *Wall Street Journal*, December 5, 2011.

9. Ibid.

10. Kerri Smith, CEO, BellyRest, interview with the author, November 11, 2012.

CHAPTER 7: CONTRIBUTE

1. Ron Ruggless, "Panera Cares Cafe Opens in Chicago," *Nation's Restaurant News*, June 21, 2012, http://nrn.com/latest-headlines/panera-cares-caf-opens-chicago.

2. Ibid.

3. Robert Gertner, interview with Niala Boodhoo, "Panera Sandwich Chain Explores 'Pay What You Want' Concept," *Morning Edition*, September 7, 2012, http://m.npr.org/story/160685977.

4. Ibid.

5. AMP Agency and Cone Communications, "Cone Millennial Case Study," 2006, http://www.conecomm.com/2006-millennial-cause-study.

6. http://purpose.edelman.com/slides/introducing-goodpurpose-2012/.

7. http://www.marketresearch.com/Mintel-International-Group-Ltd -v614/Moms-7086258.

8. M2Moms.com, "Fast Facts: Explore the State of Mom," http://www .m2moms.com/fast_facts.php.

9. David Vogel, "CSR Doesn't Pay," *Forbes*, October 16, 2008.

10. Scott Medintz, "Clinton Global Initiative: Can Companies Be Good and Do Well?" *Time*, September 25, 2012.

11. Ibid.

12. Ibid.

13. TOMS, "Blake Mycoskie," http://www.toms.com/blakes-bio.

14. TOMS, "Toms Eyewear," http://www.toms.com/eyewear/our-movement.

15. David Hessekiel, "Ad Age," February 10, 2012, http://adage.com /article/goodworks/influential-marketing-campaigns/142037.

16. Jennifer LaRue Huget, "Is Buying KFC by the Bucket a Good Way to Fight Breast Cancer?" *Washington Post*, May 4, 2010.

17. Anne Landman, "Can Eating Junk Food Cure Breast Cancer?" *PR Watch*, April 21, 2010, http://www.prwatch.org/news/2010/04/9017 /can-eating-junk-food-cure-breast-cancer.

18. B Corporation, http://www.bcorporation.net/index.php.

19. Ibid.

20. Jay Coen Gilbert, "TedX Philadelphia," December 8, 2012.

21. http://www.esquire.com/blogs/politics/benefit-corporation-law -082510.

22. AMP Agency and Cone Communications, "Cone Millennial Case Study."

23. http://www.deloitte.com/view/en_GX/global/about/global-initiatives /world-economic-forum/annual-meeting-at-davos/8182b8e049b3c3 10VgnVCM3000003456f70aRCRD.htm#.UUZISRlP3zV.

24. Jay Coen Gilbert, "TedX Philadelphia," December 8, 2012.

25. Freelancers Insurance Company, http://freelancersinsuranceco.com /fic/about-us/index.

26. Sungevity, http://www.sungevity.com/.

27. http://betterworldbook.com/.

28. Cone Communications, "2010 Cause Evolution Study," http://www
.conecomm.com/2010-cone-cause-evolution-study.

29. Richard Eisenberg, "Companies That Care: Brands That Give Back,"
Ladies Home Journal, http://www.lhj.com/volunteering/companies
-that-care-brands-that-give-back/.

30. Wendy Winks, executive director, Rock School Scholarship Fund,
interview with the author, November 30, 2012.

31. Carrie Norton, founder, Green Business Base Camp, interview with
the author, November 27, 2012.

SUMMATION

1. Katie Stagliano, interview with the author, December 4, 2012.

INDEX